light and easy

100 EASY RECIPES
light and easy

bay books

contents

soups

chicken noodle and mushroom soup

cooking oil spray
2 teaspoons grated fresh ginger
4 spring onions (scallions), finely chopped
1 boneless, skinless chicken breast, cut into
   thin strips
120 g (4 oz) button mushrooms, sliced
410 g (14 oz) tin chicken consommé
60 g (2 oz) instant noodles
3 teaspoons kecap manis (see Note)

serves 6

method Heat a little oil in a saucepan, add the ginger, spring onion and chicken and stir-fry over high heat for 4–5 minutes, or until the chicken changes colour. Add the mushrooms and stir-fry for a further 1 minute.

Add the consommé and 500 ml (17 fl oz/2 cups) water and bring to the boil. Stir in the noodles, then reduce the heat and simmer for 3 minutes, or until the noodles are soft. Stir in the kecap manis.

note *Kecap manis is a thick, sweet soy sauce available from Asian grocery stores. If you cannot find it, use regular soy sauce with a little soft brown sugar added, as a substitute.*

seafood ravioli in gingery soup

8 raw prawns (shrimp), about 250 g (9 oz)
1 carrot, chopped
1 onion, chopped
1 celery stalk, chopped
3 spring onions (scallions), thinly sliced
6 cm (2½ inch) piece fresh ginger,
thinly shredded
1 tablespoon mirin
1 teaspoon kecap manis
(see Note, page 8)
1 tablespoon soy sauce
4 large scallops
100 g (4 oz) boneless white fish fillet
1 egg white
200 g (7 oz) gow gee wrappers
1 handful coriander (cilantro) leaves

serves 4

method To make the soup, peel and devein the prawns, reserve four for the ravioli filling and chop the rest into small pieces and reserve. Put the prawn heads and shells in a large frying pan, cook over high heat until starting to brown, then cover with 1 litre (35 fl oz/4 cups) water. Add the carrot, onion and celery, bring to the boil, reduce the heat and simmer for 10 minutes. Strain and discard the prawn heads, shells and vegetables. Return the stock to a clean pan and add the spring onion, ginger, mirin, kecap manis and soy sauce. Set aside.

To make the ravioli, chop the whole reserved prawns with the scallops and fish in a food processor until smooth. Add enough egg white to bind. Lay half the round wrappers on a work surface and place a rounded teaspoon of filling in the centre of each. Brush the edges with water. Top each with another wrapper and press the edges to seal, eliminating air bubbles as you go. Trim with a fluted cutter. Cover with plastic wrap.

Bring a large saucepan of water to the boil. Meanwhile, heat the stock and leave it simmering. Just before serving, drop a few ravioli at a time into the boiling water. Cook for 2 minutes, remove with a slotted spoon and divide among heated bowls. Cook the chopped reserved prawns in the same water for 2 minutes; drain. Pour the hot stock over the ravioli and serve, sprinkled with the chopped cooked prawns and coriander leaves.

potato, broccoli and coriander soup

500 g (1 lb 2 oz) broccoli
cooking oil spray
2 onions, finely chopped
2 garlic cloves, finely chopped
2 teaspoons ground cumin
1 teaspoon ground coriander
750 g (1 lb 10 oz) potatoes, cubed
2 small chicken stock cubes
375 ml (13 fl oz/1½ cups) skim milk
3 tablespoons finely chopped coriander
   (cilantro)

serves 6

method Cut the broccoli into small pieces. Lightly spray the base of a large saucepan with oil, then place over medium heat and add the onion and garlic. Add 1 tablespoon water to prevent sticking. Cover and cook, stirring occasionally, over low heat for 5 minutes, or until the onion has softened and is lightly golden. Add the ground cumin and coriander and cook for 2 minutes.

Add the potato and broccoli to the pan, stir well and add the stock cubes and 1 litre (35 fl oz/4 cups) water. Slowly bring to the boil, reduce the heat, cover and simmer over low heat for 20 minutes, or until the vegetables are tender. Allow to cool slightly.

Blend the soup in batches in a food processor or blender until smooth. Return to the pan and stir in the milk. Slowly reheat, without boiling. Stir the chopped coriander through and season well before serving.

minestrone

250 g (9 oz) dried borlotti beans
2 tablespoons olive oil
2 onions, chopped
2 garlic cloves, crushed
90 g (3 oz) bacon slices, chopped
4 roma (plum) tomatoes, peeled and chopped
3 tablespoons chopped parsley
2 litres (8 cups) beef or vegetable stock
3 tablespoons red wine
1 carrot, chopped
1 swede (rutabaga), peeled and diced
2 potatoes, cubed
3 tablespoons tomato paste
(concentrated purée)
2 zucchini (courgettes), sliced
90 g (3 oz/$\frac{2}{3}$ cup) peas
90 g (3 oz) small macaroni
parmesan cheese, to serve

serves 8

method Soak the borlotti beans in water overnight then drain. Add to a saucepan of boiling water, simmer for 15 minutes, then drain. Heat the oil in a large heavy-based pan and cook the onion, garlic and bacon pieces until the onion is soft and the bacon golden.

Add the tomato, parsley, borlotti beans, stock and red wine. Simmer, covered, over low heat for 2 hours. Add the carrot, swede, potato and tomato paste, cover and simmer for a further 15–20 minutes. Add the zucchini, peas and pasta. Cover and simmer for 10–15 minutes, or until the vegetables and macaroni are tender. Season and serve with a little grated parmesan.

hint *For a lighter taste, use chicken stock instead of the beef stock and omit the bacon.*

tom yam goong

500 g (1 lb 2 oz) raw prawns (shrimp)
1 tablespoon oil
2 tablespoons tom yam curry paste
2 tablespoons tamarind purée
2 teaspoons ground turmeric
1 teaspoon chopped small red chillies
4 makrut (kaffir lime) leaves, shredded,
    plus extra, to garnish
2 tablespoons fish sauce
2 tablespoons lime juice
2 teaspoons grated palm sugar (jaggery)
    or soft brown sugar

serves 6

method Peel the prawns, leaving the tails intact. Reserve the shells and heads. Devein the prawns, starting at the head end. Cover and refrigerate the prawn meat. Heat the oil in a wok or large saucepan and cook the shells and heads over medium heat, stirring frequently, for 10 minutes, or until the shells turn orange.

Add 250 ml (9 fl oz/1 cup) of water and the tom yam paste to the pan. Bring to the boil and cook for 5 minutes, or until reduced slightly. Add another 2 litres (8 cups) water, bring to the boil, reduce the heat and simmer for 20 minutes. Strain, discarding the shells and heads. Return the stock to the pan.

Add the tamarind purée, turmeric, red chilli and makrut leaves to the pan, bring to the boil and cook for 2 minutes. Add the prawn meat and cook for 5 minutes, or until pink. Stir in the fish sauce, lime juice and sugar. Garnish with shredded makrut leaves.

roasted red capsicum soup

4 large red capsicums (peppers)
4 ripe tomatoes
2 tablespoons oil
1 red onion, chopped
1 garlic clove, crushed
1 litre (35 fl oz/4 cups) vegetable stock
1 teaspoon sweet chilli sauce
parmesan cheese and pesto, to serve
(optional)

serves 6

method Cut the capsicums into large flat pieces, removing the seeds and membrane. Place skin side up under a hot grill (broiler) until blackened. Leave covered with a tea towel (dish towel) until cool, then peel away the skin and chop the flesh.

Score a small cross in the base of each tomato, put them in a large heatproof bowl and cover with boiling water. Leave for 1 minute, then plunge into cold water and peel the skin from the cross. Cut in half, scoop out the seeds and roughly chop the flesh.

Heat the oil in a large heavy-based saucepan over medium heat. Cook the onion for 10 minutes, stirring frequently, until very soft. Add the garlic and cook for a further 1 minute. Add the capsicum, tomato and stock; bring to the boil, reduce the heat and simmer for about 20 minutes.

Purée the soup in a food processor or blender until smooth (in batches if necessary). Return to the pan to reheat gently and stir in the chilli sauce. Serve topped with shavings of parmesan and a little pesto, if desired.

won ton noodle soup

70 g (3 oz) raw prawns (shrimp)
70 g (3 oz) minced (ground) veal
3 tablespoons soy sauce
1 tablespoon finely chopped spring
  onion (scallion)
1 tablespoon finely chopped water chestnuts
1 teaspoon finely chopped fresh ginger
2 garlic cloves, finely chopped
24 gow gee wrappers
1.25 litres (5 cups) chicken stock
2 tablespoons mirin
500 g (1 lb 2 oz) baby bok choy
  (pak choy), finely shredded
8 spring onions (scallions), sliced

serves 4

method Peel, devein and finely chop the prawns. Mix with the minced veal, 2 teaspoons soy sauce, spring onion, water chestnuts, ginger and garlic. Lay the round wrappers out on a work surface and place a teaspoon of mixture in the middle of each.

Moisten the edges of the wrappers and bring up the sides to form a pouch. Pinch together to seal. Cook in batches in a large saucepan of rapidly boiling water for 4–5 minutes. Drain and divide among bowls.

Bring the stock, remaining soy sauce and mirin to the boil in a large saucepan. Add the bok choy, cover and simmer for 2 minutes, or until the bok choy has just wilted. Add the sliced spring onion and season. Ladle the stock, bok choy and spring onion over the won tons.

curried sweet potato soup

1 tablespoon oil
1 large onion, chopped
2 garlic cloves, crushed
3 teaspoons curry powder
1.25 kg (2 lb 12 oz) orange sweet potato,
peeled and cubed
1 litre (35 fl oz/4 cups) chicken stock
1 large apple, peeled, cored and grated
125 ml (4 fl oz/½ cup) light coconut milk

serves 6

method   Heat the oil in a large saucepan over medium heat and cook the onion for 10 minutes, stirring occasionally, until very soft. Add the garlic and curry powder and cook for a further 1 minute.

Add the sweet potato, stock and apple. Bring to the boil, reduce the heat and simmer, partially covered, for 30 minutes, until very soft.

Cool the soup a little before processing in batches until smooth. Return to the pan, stir in the coconut milk and reheat gently without boiling. Serve with warm pitta bread.

note   *Can be kept in the fridge for 1 day without the coconut milk: add this when you reheat.*

hot and sour lime soup with beef

1 litre (35 fl oz/4 cups) beef stock
2 lemongrass stems, white part only, halved
3 garlic cloves, halved
2.5 cm (1 inch) piece fresh ginger, sliced
3 very large handfuls coriander (cilantro),
 leaves and stalks separated
4 spring onions (scallions), thinly sliced
2 strips lime zest
2 star anise
3 small fresh red chillies, seeded and
 finely chopped
500 g (1 lb 2 oz) fillet steak, trimmed
2 tablespoons fish sauce
1 tablespoon grated palm sugar (jaggery)
2 tablespoons lime juice, or to taste
coriander (cilantro) leaves, to garnish

serves 4

method Put the stock, lemongrass, garlic, ginger, coriander stalks, half the spring onion, lime zest, star anise, 1 teaspoon chopped chilli and 1 litre (35 fl oz/4 cups) water in a saucepan. Bring to the boil and simmer, covered, for 25 minutes. Strain and return the liquid to the pan.

Heat a chargrill pan or barbecue flat plate until very hot. Brush lightly with olive oil and sear the steak on both sides until browned but very rare in the centre.

Reheat the soup, adding the fish sauce and palm sugar. Season with salt and black pepper. Add the lime juice to taste (you may want more than 2 tablespoons) to achieve a hot and sour flavour.

Add the remaining spring onion and the chopped coriander leaves to the soup. Slice the beef across the grain into thin strips. Curl the strips into a decorative pattern, then place in the centre of four deep wide serving bowls. Pour the soup over the beef and garnish with the remaining chilli and a few extra coriander leaves.

chicken and couscous soup

1 tablespoon olive oil
1 onion, sliced
½ teaspoon ground cumin
½ teaspoon paprika
1 teaspoon grated fresh ginger
1 garlic clove, crushed
2 celery stalks, sliced
2 small carrots, sliced
2 zucchini (courgettes), sliced
1.25 litres (5 cups) chicken stock
2 boneless, skinless chicken breasts, sliced
pinch saffron threads, optional
95 g (3 oz/½ cup) instant couscous
2 tablespoons chopped flat-leaf
(Italian) parsley

serves 6

method   Heat the oil in a large heavy-based saucepan. Add the onion and cook over medium heat for 10 minutes, or until very soft, stirring occasionally. Add the cumin, paprika, ginger and garlic and cook, stirring, for 1 minute further.

Add the celery, carrot and zucchini and stir to coat with the spices. Stir in the stock. Bring to the boil, then reduce the heat and simmer, partially covered, for 15 minutes, or until the vegetables are tender.

Add the chicken and saffron to the pan and cook for about 5 minutes, or until the chicken is just tender; do not overcook. Stir in the couscous and chopped parsley and serve.

hint   *Add the couscous to the soup just before serving because it absorbs liquid quickly and will become very thick.*

salads

pesto beef salad

100 g (4 oz) button mushrooms
1 large yellow capsicum (pepper)
1 large red capsicum (pepper)
cooking oil spray
100 g (4 oz) lean fillet steak
135 g (5 oz/1½ cups) penne

pesto

3 very large handfuls basil leaves, plus extra,
 to serve
2 garlic cloves, chopped
2 tablespoons pepitas (pumpkin seeds)
1 tablespoon olive oil
2 tablespoons orange juice
1 tablespoon lemon juice

serves 8

method Cut the mushrooms into quarters. Cut the capsicums into large flat pieces, removing the seeds and membrane. Place skin side up under a hot grill (broiler) until blackened. Cover with a tea towel (dish towel) until cool, then peel away the skin and chop the flesh.

Spray a non-stick frying pan with oil and cook the steak over high heat for 3–4 minutes each side until medium-rare. Remove and leave for 5 minutes before cutting into thin slices. Season with a little salt.

To make the pesto, finely chop the basil, garlic and pepitas in a food processor. With the motor running, add the oil, orange and lemon juice. Season well.

Meanwhile, cook the penne in a large pan of rapidly boiling salted water until al dente. Drain, then toss with the pesto in a large bowl. Add the capsicum pieces, steak slices, mushroom quarters and basil leaves to the penne and toss to distribute evenly. Serve immediately.

roast pumpkin and onion with rocket

800 g (1 lb 12 oz) peeled jap pumpkin
(winter squash)
2 small red onions
2 garlic cloves, finely chopped
cooking oil spray
150 g (5 oz) rocket (arugula)
balsamic vinegar, to drizzle

serves 4

method   Preheat the oven to 200°C (400°F/Gas 6). Cut the pumpkin into 3 cm (1¼ inch) cubes and cut the onions into small wedges. Line a baking dish with baking paper, add the vegetables and sprinkle with the garlic. Lightly spray with oil. Season and cook for 30–35 minutes, or until the pumpkin is just tender. Set aside.

Tear the leaves from the rocket into pieces. Arrange on a platter, then top with the pumpkin and onion. Drizzle all over with the balsamic vinegar. Serve warm.

chicken and cabbage salad

3 boneless, skinless chicken breasts
1 red chilli, seeded and finely chopped
3 tablespons lime juice
2 tablespoons soft brown sugar
3 tablespons fish sauce
½ Chinese cabbage, shredded
2 carrots, grated
50 g (2 oz/1 bunch) shredded mint

serves 4

method Put the chicken in a saucepan, cover with water and bring to the boil, then reduce the heat and simmer for 10 minutes, or until cooked through.

While the chicken is cooking, combine the chilli, lime juice, sugar and fish sauce. Remove the chicken from the water. Cool slightly, then shred into small pieces.

Combine the chicken, cabbage, carrot, mint and dressing. Toss well and serve immediately.

lime and prawn salad

200 g (7 oz) baby green beans
2 Lebanese (short) cucumbers, sliced
4 spring onions (scallions), finely chopped
1 tablespoon finely shredded makrut
(kaffir lime) leaves
3 tablespoons flaked coconut
750 g (1 lb 10 oz) cooked prawns (shrimp),
peeled and deveined, tails intact
2 teaspoons shredded lime zest

dressing

1 tablespoon peanut oil
1 tablespoon nam pla (Thai fish sauce)
1 tablespoon grated palm sugar (jaggery)
1 tablespoon chopped coriander (cilantro)
2 teaspoons soy sauce
1–2 teaspoons sweet chilli sauce
3 tablespoons lime juice

serves 4

method   Cook the beans in a small saucepan of boiling water for 2 minutes. Drain and cover with cold water, then drain again and pat dry with paper towels.

To make the dressing, whisk all the ingredients in a bowl.

Combine the beans, cucumber, spring onion, makrut leaves, flaked coconut and prawns in a large bowl. Add the dressing and toss gently to combine. Place the salad in a large serving bowl and garnish with the shredded lime zest.

note   *Young lemon leaves can be used in place of the makrut leaves. Soft brown or dark brown sugar may be substituted for the palm sugar.*

thai-spiced pork and green mango salad

2 stems lemongrass, white part only,
   thinly sliced
1 garlic clove
2 red Asian shallots
1 tablespoon coarsely chopped fresh ginger
1 red bird's eye chilli, seeded
1 tablespoon fish sauce
1 large handful coriander (cilantro), plus
   3 tablespoons chopped leaves
1 teaspoon grated lime zest
1 tablespoon lime juice
2 tablespoons oil
2 pork tenderloins, trimmed
2 green mangoes, cut into matchsticks
1 carrot, grated
45 g (1½ oz/½ cup) bean sprouts, trimmed
½ red onion, thinly sliced
3 tablespoons chopped mint
3 tablespoons chopped Vietnamese mint

dressing

1 large red chilli, seeded and finely chopped
2 garlic cloves, finely chopped
3 coriander (cilantro) roots, finely chopped
1¼ tablespoons grated palm sugar (jaggery)
2 tablespoons fish sauce
3 tablespoons lime juice

serves 4

method Place the lemongrass, garlic, shallots, ginger, chilli, fish sauce, lime zest, lime juice, oil and 1 large handful coriander in a blender or food processor and process until a coarse paste forms. Transfer to a non-metallic dish. Coat the pork in the marinade, cover and refrigerate for at least 2 hours, but no longer than 4 hours.

To make the dressing, mix all the ingredients together in a bowl.

Combine the mango, carrot, bean sprouts, red onion, mint, Vietnamese mint and remaining coriander in a large bowl.

Preheat a grill (broiler) or a chargrill pan and cook the pork over medium heat for 4–5 minutes each side, until cooked through. Remove from the heat, and then leave to rest for 5 minutes before slicing to serve.

Toss the dressing and salad together. Season to taste with salt and cracked black pepper. Arrange the pork in a circle in the centre of each plate and top with salad. Delicious with steamed jasmine rice.

tandoori lamb salad

250 g (9 oz/1 cup) low-fat plain yoghurt
2 garlic cloves, crushed
2 teaspoons grated fresh ginger
2 teaspoons ground turmeric
2 teaspoons garam masala
¼ teaspoon paprika
2 teaspoons ground coriander
red food colouring (optional)
500 g (1 lb 2 oz) lean lamb fillets
4 tablespoons lemon juice
1½ teaspoons chopped coriander (cilantro)
1 teaspoon chopped mint
150 g (5 oz) mixed salad leaves
1 large mango, cut into strips
2 Lebanese (short) cucumbers, cut into strips

serves 4

method Mix the yoghurt, garlic, ginger and spices in a bowl, add a little colouring (if using) and toss with the lamb to thoroughly coat. Cover and refrigerate overnight.

Grill the lamb on a foil-lined baking tray under high heat for 7 minutes each side, or until the marinade starts to brown. Set aside for 5 minutes before serving.

Mix the lemon juice, coriander and mint, then season. Toss with the salad leaves, mango and cucumber, then arrange on plates. Slice the lamb and serve over the salad.

citrus fruit and rocket salad

1 grapefruit
2 small red grapefruit
4 oranges
1 red onion, sliced
1 large handful coriander (cilantro) leaves
2 tablespoons honey
4 tablespoons raspberry vinegar
150 g (5 oz) rocket (arugula)

serves 6

method Remove the zest from the grapefruits and oranges. Remove and discard all the pith from a few slices of the zest from each fruit and cut the zest into long thin strips. Remove any remaining pith from the fruit and slice between each section. Segment the fruit over a bowl to catch any juice, then set the juice aside.

Put the segments and zest in a salad bowl with the onion and coriander leaves. Add the honey and raspberry vinegar to the reserved fruit juice and whisk to combine. Pour over the salad and toss. Serve on a bed of rocket.

100 EASY RECIPES LIGHT AND EASY

thai beef salad with mint and coriander

2 tablespoons dried shrimp
125 g (5 oz) English spinach
1 tablespoon sesame oil
500 g (1 lb 2 oz) rump steak
90 g (3 oz/1 cup) bean sprouts, trimmed
1 small red onion, thinly sliced
1 small red capsicum (pepper),
cut into thin strips
1 small Lebanese (short) cucumber,
cut into thin strips
200 g (7 oz) daikon radish, peeled
and cut into thin strips
1 small tomato, halved, seeded and
thinly sliced
1 handful mint leaves
1 very large handful coriander
(cilantro) leaves
2 garlic cloves, finely chopped
1–2 small red chillies, chopped
2 small green chillies, chopped

dressing

3 tablespoons lime juice
3 tablespoons fish sauce
1 tablespoon finely chopped lemongrass
1 teaspoon sugar

serves 6

method   Soak the dried shrimp in hot water for 15 minutes; drain well and chop finely. Wash the English spinach and drain well. Trim the thick stalks and coarsely shred the leaves.

Heat the oil in a frying pan, add the steak and cook over high heat for 1½–2 minutes on each side until medium-rare. Allow to cool slightly and then slice the steak thinly.

To make the dressing, combine the lime juice, fish sauce, lemongrass and sugar in a small bowl. Whisk until the ingredients are well combined.

To serve, combine the shrimp, sliced beef, bean sprouts, onion, capsicum, cucumber, radish, tomato, mint, coriander, garlic and chillies in a large bowl. Place the spinach on a serving plate, top with the combined beef and vegetables, and drizzle with the dressing.

chargrilled tuna and ruby grapefruit salad

4 ruby grapefruit
cooking oil spray
3 tuna steaks
150 g (5 oz) rocket (arugula) leaves
1 red onion, sliced

dressing

2 tablespoons almond oil
2 tablespoons raspberry vinegar
½ teaspoon sugar
1 tablespoon shredded mint

serves 6

method   Cut a slice off each end of the grapefruit and peel away the skin, removing all the pith. Separate the segments and set aside in a bowl.

Heat a barbecue grill plate or flat plate and spray lightly with oil. Cook each tuna steak for 3–4 minutes on each side. This will leave the centre slightly pink. Cool, then thinly slice.

To make the dressing, put the almond oil, vinegar, sugar and mint in a small screw-top jar and shake until well combined.

Place the rocket on a serving plate and top with the grapefruit segments, then the tuna and onion. Drizzle with the dressing and serve.

100 EASY RECIPES LIGHT AND EASY

tofu salad with ginger miso dressing

90 ml (3 fl oz) light soy sauce
2 teaspoons soy bean oil
2 garlic cloves, crushed
1 teaspoon grated fresh ginger
1 teaspoon chilli paste
500 g (1 lb 2 oz) firm tofu, cut into
small cubes
400 g (14 oz) mesclun leaves
1 Lebanese (short) cucumber, finely sliced
250 g (9 oz) cherry tomatoes, halved
2 teaspoons soy bean oil, extra

dressing

2 teaspoons white miso paste (see Note)
2 tablespoons mirin
1 teaspoon sesame oil
1 teaspoon grated fresh ginger
1 teaspoon finely snipped chives
1 tablespoon toasted sesame seeds

serves 4

method   Mix together the light soy sauce, soy bean oil, garlic, ginger, chilli paste and $1/2$ teaspoon salt in a bowl. Add the tofu and mix until well coated. Marinate for at least 10 minutes, or preferably overnight. Drain and reserve the marinade.

To make the dressing, combine the miso with 125 ml (4 fl oz/$1/2$ cup) hot water and leave until the miso dissolves. Add the mirin, sesame oil, ginger, chives and sesame seeds and stir until beginning to thicken.

Put the mesclun leaves, cucumber and tomato in a serving bowl.

Heat the extra soy bean oil on a chargrill plate or flat plate. Add the tofu and cook over medium heat for 4 minutes, or until golden brown. Pour on the reserved marinade and cook for a further 1 minute over high heat. Remove from the grill and cool for 5 minutes.

Add the tofu to the salad, drizzle with the dressing and toss well.

note   *Miso is Japanese bean paste and is commonly used in soups, dressings, on grilled foods and as a flavouring for pickles.*

japanese king prawn and noodle salad

500 g (1 lb 2 oz) fresh udon noodles
2 teaspoons sesame oil
3 garlic cloves, finely chopped
4 cm (1½ inch) piece ginger, finely chopped
200 g (7 oz) broccoli, cut into small pieces
2 carrots, cut into matchsticks
100 g (4 oz) snow peas (mangetouts), sliced
    into long, thin strips
90 g (3 oz/1 cup) bean sprouts, trimmed
1 large handful coriander (cilantro), chopped
2 tablespoons mirin
3 tablespoons low-salt soy sauce
8 cooked king prawns (shrimp), peeled and
    deveined, tails intact
2 teaspoons sesame seeds, toasted
sliced spring onions (scallions), to garnish

serves 6

method Cook the udon noodles in a large pan of boiling water for 5 minutes, or until tender. Drain and rinse in cold water to prevent them sticking together. Transfer to a large bowl and cut into small pieces, using scissors. Toss 1 teaspoon of the sesame oil through, cover and set aside.

Heat the remaining sesame oil in a small frying pan, add the garlic and ginger and cook over low heat for 5 minutes, stirring occasionally. Remove from the heat, cool and add to the noodles.

Bring a large saucepan of water to the boil and add the broccoli, carrot and snow peas. Return to the boil, reduce the heat and simmer for 1 minute. Rinse under cold water until the vegetables are cold. Drain well.

Add the blanched vegetables, bean sprouts, coriander, mirin, soy sauce and prawns to the noodles. Toss together until well combined. Transfer to a serving bowl and sprinkle with sesame seeds and spring onion. Serve immediately.

note *Udon noodles and mirin are available from Japanese or Asian food stores and some supermarkets.*

spicy pork salad

1 tablespoon oil
500 g (1 lb 2 oz) minced (ground) pork
2 tablespoons fish sauce
1 tablespoon soy sauce
2½ tablespoons lime juice
1 tablespoon soft brown sugar
10 spring onions (scallions), finely chopped
3 lemongrass stems, white part only,
finely chopped
2 red chillies, seeded and sliced
2 tablespoons chopped coriander (cilantro)
2 tablespoons chopped mint
2 tablespoons chopped parsley
lettuce leaves, for serving

serves 6

method   Heat the oil in a frying pan. Add the pork and cook over medium–high heat for 10 minutes, or until well browned, breaking up any lumps with a fork as it cooks. Remove from the pan and leave to cool.

Combine the sauces, lime juice and brown sugar in a bowl. Add the pork, then mix in the spring onion, lemongrass, chilli and fresh herbs.

Cover and refrigerate for at least 3 hours, stirring occasionally, or overnight. To serve, lay a lettuce leaf on each plate and spoon in some of the pork mixture.

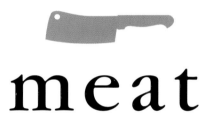

meat

indian-style lamb couscous

250 g (9 oz) lamb backstrap (tender eye fillet
  of the lamb loin)
1 tablespoon mild curry powder
2 tablespoons pepitas (pumpkin seeds)
2 tablespoons sesame seeds
2 teaspoons cumin seeds
2 teaspoons coriander seeds
1 tablespoon oil
2 tablespoons lemon juice, plus extra, to serve
1 onion, chopped
1 carrot, chopped
125 g (5 oz) orange sweet potato, cubed
1 garlic clove, finely chopped
185 g (7 oz/1 cup) couscous
40 g (1½ oz/⅓ cup) raisins

serves 6

method   Sprinkle the lamb with the combined curry powder and a pinch of salt, then turn to coat well. Cover with plastic wrap and refrigerate.

Place the pepitas and sesame seeds in a dry frying pan and cook, stirring, over medium–high heat until the seeds begin to brown. Add the cumin and coriander seeds and continue stirring until the pepitas are puffed up. Remove from the heat and allow to cool.

Heat the oil in a frying pan, add the lamb and cook over medium–high heat for 5–8 minutes, or until browned. Remove from the pan, drizzle with half the lemon and leave to cool to room temperature. Turn the meat occasionally to coat in the juice while cooling.

Reheat the pan over high heat and stir the onion, carrot and sweet potato until the onion is translucent. Reduce the heat to medium, add 3 tablespoons water, cover and cook for about 3 minutes, or until the vegetables are tender. Stir in the garlic and remaining lemon juice.

Pour 250 ml (9 fl oz/1 cup) boiling water into a heatproof bowl. Add the couscous. Stir until combined. Leave for 2 minutes, until the water has been absorbed. Fluff gently with a fork to separate the grains. Add the vegetable mixture, raisins and most of the toasted seeds, reserving some to sprinkle over the top, and toss until just combined. Spoon the mixture onto a serving plate. Slice the lamb thinly and arrange over the mixture. Drizzle with the extra lemon juice and sprinkle with the seeds.

pork with pear and coriander salsa

3 beurre bosc pears
3–4 tablespoons lime juice
1 red onion, finely diced
2 large handfuls coriander (cilantro) leaves,
finely chopped
½ teaspoon chilli flakes
1 teaspoon finely grated lime zest
cooking oil spray
4 pork steaks, butterflied

serves 4

method Cut the pears into quarters, remove the cores and chop into small dice. Sprinkle with the lime juice. Combine the pear, onion, coriander, chilli flakes and lime zest and season.

Lightly spray a frying pan with oil and cook the pork steaks for 5 minutes on each side, or until cooked through. Serve with the salsa.

note *Use pears that are just ready to eat, not overripe or floury fruit.*

beef with mango, raisin and tomato salsa

2 tomatoes
1 mango
60 g (2 oz/½ cup) raisins
1 teaspoon tinned green peppercorns,
    drained and crushed
1 teaspoon finely grated lemon zest
2 tablespoons red wine vinegar
1 tablespoon olive oil
1 spring onion (scallion), shredded
750 g (1 lb 10 oz) piece eye fillet beef

serves 4

method Preheat the oven to 180°C (350°F/Gas 4). Score a cross in the base of each tomato. Place in a bowl of boiling water for 10 seconds, then plunge into cold water and peel the skin away from the cross. Scoop out the seeds and discard. Finely chop the tomato flesh and put in a bowl.

Peel and finely dice the mango and mix with the tomato and raisins. Mix together the peppercorns, lemon zest, vinegar and oil and add to the salsa. Season and scatter with spring onion.

Place the beef in a lightly oiled roasting tin and roast in the oven for 30–35 minutes. Stand for 10 minutes before slicing.

pasta all'arrabbiata

4 double-smoked bacon slices, rind removed
2 teaspoons olive oil
4 red chillies, seeded and chopped
2 large onions, finely chopped
3 garlic cloves, crushed
800 g (1 lb 12 oz) very ripe tomatoes,
finely chopped
500 g (1 lb 2 oz) lasagnette pasta
2 tablespoons chopped parsley
grated parmesan cheese, to serve

serves 4

method Chop the bacon. Heat the olive oil in a heavy-based saucepan and add the bacon, chilli, onion and garlic. Cook over medium heat for about 8 minutes, stirring occasionally.

Add the tomato and 3 tablespoons water to the pan and season to taste with salt and pepper. Simmer, covered, for about 40 minutes, or until the sauce is thick and rich.

Cook the pasta in a large saucepan of rapidly boiling water until al dente. Drain and rinse thoroughly in a colander, then return the pasta to the pan and keep warm.

Add the parsley to the sauce and season again if necessary. Pour the sauce over the pasta, tossing to coat the pasta thoroughly. Serve sprinkled with a little grated parmesan.

note *Good-quality bacon and very ripe, full-flavoured tomatoes are essential to the flavour of this dish.*

burmese pork curry

2 lemongrass stems, white part only, sliced
1 red onion, chopped
1 garlic clove
1 teaspoon grated fresh ginger
2 large red dried chillies
1 teaspoon fenugreek seeds, roasted
and ground
1 teaspoon yellow mustard seeds, roasted
and ground
2 teaspoons paprika
2 tablespoons worcestershire sauce
750 g (1 lb 10 oz) lean boneless shoulder
of pork, cut into cubes
2 tablespoons fish sauce
6 new potatoes, peeled and sliced
2 small red onions, diced
1 tablespoon olive oil
2 tablespoons mango chutney

serves 6

method Put the lemongrass, onion, garlic, ginger, chillies, fenugreek seeds, mustard seeds, paprika and sauce in a food processor or blender and mix to a thick paste.

Place the pork in a bowl, sprinkle with the fish sauce and $1/4$ teaspoon ground black pepper.

Place the potato and onion in another bowl, add 3 tablespoons of the paste and toss to coat. Add the remaining paste to the pork. Mix well.

Heat the oil in a frying pan or wok over medium heat. Add the pork and cook in batches, stirring, for 8 minutes, or until it begins to brown. Remove from the pan. Add the potato and onion. Cook, stirring, for 5 minutes, or until soft and starting to brown.

Return the meat to the pan and stir in 750 ml (26 fl oz/3 cups) water, adding 250 ml (9 fl oz/1 cup) at a time. Stir in the mango chutney, then reduce the heat and simmer for 30 minutes.

rogan josh

1 kg (2 lb 4 oz) boned leg of lamb
1 tablespoon oil
2 onions, chopped
125 g (5 oz/½ cup) low-fat plain yoghurt
1 teaspoon chilli powder
1 tablespoon ground coriander
2 teaspoons ground cumin
1 teaspoon ground cardamom
½ teaspoon ground cloves
1 teaspoon ground turmeric
3 garlic cloves, crushed
1 tablespoon grated fresh ginger
400 g (14 oz) tin chopped tomatoes
3 tablepoons slivered almonds
1 teaspoon garam masala
chopped coriander (cilantro) leaves, for serving

serves 6

method Trim the lamb of any fat or sinew and cut into small cubes.

Heat the oil in a large saucepan, add the onion and cook, stirring, for 5 minutes, or until soft. Stir in the yoghurt, chilli powder, coriander, cumin, cardamom, cloves, turmeric, garlic and ginger. Add the tomato and 1 teaspoon salt and simmer for 5 minutes.

Add the lamb and stir until coated. Cover and cook over low heat, stirring occasionally, for 1–1½ hours, or until the lamb is tender. Uncover and simmer until the liquid thickens.

Meanwhile, toast the almonds in a dry frying pan over medium heat for 3–4 minutes, shaking the pan gently, until the nuts are golden. Remove from the pan at once to prevent them burning.

Add the garam masala to the curry and mix through well. Sprinkle the slivered almonds and coriander leaves over the top and serve.

beef lasagne

2 teaspoons olive oil
1 large onion, chopped
2 carrots, finely chopped
2 celery stalks, finely chopped
2 zucchini (courgettes), finely chopped
2 garlic cloves, crushed
500 g (1 lb 2 oz) lean minced (ground) beef
2 x 400 g (14 oz) tins chopped tomatoes
125 ml (4 fl oz/½ cup) beef stock
2 tablespoons tomato paste
   (concentrated purée)
2 teaspoons dried oregano
375 g (13 oz) lasagne sheets

cheese sauce

750 ml (26 fl oz/3 cups) skim milk
40 g (1½ oz/⅓ cup) cornflour (cornstarch)
100 g (4 oz) reduced-fat cheddar cheese,
   grated

serves 8

method   Heat the olive oil in a large non-stick frying pan. Add the onion and cook until soft. Add the carrot, celery and zucchini and cook, stirring constantly, for about 5 minutes. Add the garlic and cook for another minute. Add the beef and cook over high heat, stirring, until well browned. Break up any lumps of meat.

Add the tomato, stock, tomato paste and oregano to the pan and stir to combine. Bring the mixture to the boil, reduce the heat and simmer gently, partially covered, for 20 minutes, stirring occasionally.

Preheat the oven to 180°C (350°F/Gas 4). Spread a little of the meat sauce into the base of a 23 x 30 cm (9 x 12 inch) ovenproof dish. Arrange a layer of lasagne sheets in the dish. Spread half the meat sauce over the top to cover evenly. Cover with another layer of lasagne sheets, a layer of meat sauce, then a final layer of lasagne sheets.

To make the cheese sauce, blend a little of the milk with the cornflour in a small saucepan, to form a smooth paste. Gradually blend in the remaining milk and stir constantly over low heat until the mixture boils and thickens. Remove from the heat and stir in the grated cheese until it has melted. Spread evenly over the top of the lasagne and bake for 1 hour.

Leave the lasagne to stand for 15 minutes before cutting into portions for serving.

penne with bacon, ricotta and basil

2 bacon slices
2 teaspoons olive oil
2–3 garlic cloves, crushed
1 onion, finely chopped
2 spring onions (scallions), finely chopped
250 g (9 oz/1 cup) ricotta cheese
1 very large handful basil, finely chopped
325 g (11 oz/3⅔ cups) penne
8 cherry tomatoes, halved

serves 4

method Remove the fat and rind from the bacon and chop roughly. Heat the oil in a frying pan, add the bacon, garlic, onion and spring onion and stir over medium heat for 5 minutes, or until cooked. Remove from the heat, stir in the ricotta and chopped basil and beat until smooth.

Meanwhile, cook the pasta in a large saucepan of rapidly boiling salted water for 10 minutes, or until al dente. Just prior to draining the pasta, add about 250 ml (9 fl oz/1 cup) of the pasta water to the ricotta mixture to thin the sauce. Add more water if you prefer an even thinner sauce. Season well.

Drain the pasta and stir the sauce and tomato halves into the pasta.

chilli con carne

185 g (7 oz) dried black-eyed peas
650 g (1 lb 7 oz) tomatoes
1½ tablespoons oil
900 g (2 lb) trimmed chuck steak,
    cut into cubes
3 onions, thinly sliced
2 garlic cloves, chopped
2 teaspoons ground cumin
1 tablespoon paprika
½ teaspoon ground allspice
1–2 teaspoons chilli powder
1 tablespoon soft brown sugar
1 tablespoon red wine vinegar

serves 6

method Put the peas in a bowl, cover with plenty of water and leave overnight to soak. Drain well.

Score a cross in the base of each tomato. Put the tomatoes in a bowl of boiling water for 30 seconds, then transfer to a bowl of cold water. Drain and peel the skin away from the cross. Halve the tomatoes and remove the seeds with a teaspoon. Chop the flesh finely.

Heat 1 tablespoon of the oil in a large heavy-based saucepan. Cook half the meat over medium–high heat for 2 minutes, or until well browned. Remove from the pan and repeat with the remaining meat, then remove from the pan.

Add the remaining oil to the pan and add the onion. Cook over medium heat for 5 minutes, or until softened. Add the garlic and spices and cook, stirring, for 1 minute, or until aromatic.

Add 500 ml (17 fl oz/2 cups) water and stir. Return the meat to the pan with the peas and tomato. Bring to the boil, then reduce the heat to low and simmer, partially covered, for 2 hours, or until the meat is tender and the chilli con carne is thick and dryish, stirring occasionally. Towards the end of the cooking time the mixture may start to catch, so add a little water if necessary. Stir through the sugar and vinegar, and season with salt to taste. Serve with flour tortillas, grated low-fat cheese and lime wedges.

japanese pork and noodle stir-fry

1 tablespoon oil
150 g (5 oz) pork loin, thinly sliced
5 spring onions (scallions), cut into short lengths
1 carrot, cut into thin strips
2 tablespoons Japanese soy sauce
200 g (7 oz) Chinese cabbage, shredded
500 g (1 lb 2 oz) hokkien (egg) noodles, gently pulled apart to separate
1 tablespoon worcestershire sauce
1 tablespoon mirin
2 teaspoons caster (superfine) sugar
90 g (3 oz/1 cup) bean sprouts, trimmed
1 sheet toasted nori (dried seaweed), shredded

serves 4

method   Heat the oil in a large wok over medium heat. Stir-fry the pork, spring onion and carrot for 1–2 minutes, or until the pork just changes colour.

Add the soy sauce, cabbage, noodles, worcestershire sauce, mirin, sugar and 2 tablespoons water. Cover and cook for 1 minute.

Add the bean sprouts and toss well to coat the vegetables and noodles in the sauce. Serve immediately, sprinkled with the shredded nori.

spaghetti bolognese

cooking oil spray
2 onions, finely chopped
2 garlic cloves, finely chopped
2 carrots, finely chopped
2 celery stalks, finely chopped
400 g (14 oz) lean minced (ground) beef
1 kg (2 lb 4 oz) tomatoes, chopped
125 ml (4 fl oz/½ cup) dry red wine
350 g (12 oz) spaghetti
1 very large handful parsley, finely chopped

serves 6

method Lightly spray a large saucepan with oil. Place over medium heat and add the onion, garlic, carrot and celery. Stir for 5 minutes, or until the vegetables have softened. Add 1 tablespoon water, if necessary, to prevent sticking.

Increase the heat to high, add the minced beef and cook for 5 minutes, or until browned. Stir constantly to prevent the meat sticking. Add the tomato, wine and 250 ml (9 fl oz/1 cup) water. Bring to the boil, reduce the heat and simmer, uncovered, for about 1 hour, or until the sauce has thickened.

Cook the spaghetti in a large pan of rapidly boiling salted water for 10–12 minutes, or until al dente, then drain. Stir the parsley through the sauce and season with salt and pepper. Toss the sauce through the pasta and serve immediately.

lamb cutlets with cannellini bean purée

8 lamb cutlets
4 garlic cloves
1 tablespoon chopped rosemary
2 teaspoons olive oil
2 x 400 g (14 oz) tins cannellini beans, drained
1 teaspoon ground cumin
125 ml (4 fl oz/½ cup) lemon juice
cooking oil spray
2 tablespoons balsamic vinegar

serves 4

method Trim the cutlets of excess fat from the outside edge and scrape the fat away from the bones. Place in a single layer in a shallow dish. Thinly slice 2 garlic cloves and mix with the rosemary, oil and ½ teaspoon salt and cracked black pepper. Pour over the meat, cover and refrigerate for 1 hour.

Rinse the beans and purée in a food processor with the remaining garlic, the cumin and half the lemon juice. Transfer to a saucepan, then set aside.

Lightly spray a non-stick frying pan with oil and cook the cutlets over medium heat for 1–2 minutes on each side. Add the vinegar and cook for 1 minute, turning to coat. Remove the cutlets and cover to keep warm. Add the remaining lemon juice to the pan and simmer for 2–3 minutes, or until the sauce thickens slightly. Warm the purée over medium heat and serve with the cutlets.

pork rolls with roasted capsicum

sauce

185 ml (6 fl oz/¾ cup) beef stock
2 teaspoons soy sauce
2 tablespoons dry red wine
2 teaspoons wholegrain mustard
2 teaspoons cornflour (cornstarch)

1 red capsicum (pepper)
4 x 150 g (5 oz) lean pork leg steaks
90 g (3 oz/⅓ cup) ricotta cheese
2 spring onions (scallions), finely chopped
1 garlic clove, crushed
70 g (3 oz) rocket (arugula)
4 small lean slices prosciutto (about 35 g/1 oz)
cooking oil spray

serves 4

method To make the sauce, put the beef stock, soy sauce, wine and mustard in a saucepan. Blend the cornflour with 1 tablespoon water and add to the pan. Stir until the mixture boils.

Cut the capsicum into quarters and remove the seeds and membrane. Grill (broil) until the skin blisters and blackens. Cool under a damp tea towel (dish towel), peel and cut the flesh into thin strips.

Flatten each steak into a thin square between two sheets of plastic wrap, using a rolling pin or mallet. Combine the ricotta, spring onion and garlic in a bowl, then spread evenly over the pork. Top with a layer of rocket and prosciutto. Place a quarter of the capsicum at one end and roll up to enclose the capsicum. Tie with string or secure with toothpicks at even intervals.

Spray a non-stick frying pan with oil and fry the rolls over medium heat for 5 minutes, or until they are well browned. Add the sauce and simmer over low heat for 10–15 minutes, or until the rolls are cooked. Remove the string or toothpicks. Slice and serve with the sauce.

veal cutlets in chilli tomato sauce

5 slices wholemeal (whole-wheat) bread
3 tablespoons parsley
3 garlic cloves
4 thick veal cutlets, trimmed
3 tablespoons skim milk
2 teaspoons olive oil
1 onion, finely chopped
1 tablespoon capers, drained and well rinsed
1 teaspoon tinned green peppercorns, chopped
1 teaspoon chopped red chilli
2 tablespoons balsamic vinegar
1 teaspoon soft brown sugar
2 tablespoons tomato paste (concentrated purée)
440 g (15 oz) tin chopped tomatoes

serves 4

method Preheat the oven to 180°C (350°F/Gas 4). Place a rack in a small baking dish. Chop the bread, parsley and garlic in a food processor to make fine breadcrumbs.

Season the cutlets on both sides with salt and black pepper. Pour the milk into a bowl and put the breadcrumbs on a plate. Dip the veal in the milk, then coat in the crumbs, pressing the crumbs on. Transfer to the rack and bake for 20 minutes.

While the veal is cooking, heat the oil in a small saucepan over medium heat. Add the onion, capers, peppercorns and chilli, cover and cook for 8 minutes. Mix in the vinegar, sugar and tomato paste and stir until boiling. Stir in the tomato, reduce the heat and simmer for 15 minutes.

Remove the cutlets from the rack and wipe the dish. Place the tomato sauce in the base and put the cutlets on top, and return to the oven. Reduce the oven to 150°C (300°F/Gas 2). Bake for 10 minutes to heat through.

beef pot roast

300 g (11 oz) small pickling onions
2 carrots
3 parsnips, peeled
30 g (1 oz) butter
1–1.5 kg (2 lb 4 oz–3 lb 5 oz) piece of silverside, trimmed of fat (see Note)
3 tablespoons dry red wine
1 large tomato, finely chopped
250 ml (9 fl oz/1 cup) beef stock

serves 6

method Put the onions in a heatproof bowl and cover with boiling water. Leave for 1 minute, then drain well. Allow to cool and then peel off the skins.

Cut the carrots and parsnips in half lengthways then into even-sized pieces. Heat half the butter in a large heavy-based saucepan that will tightly fit the meat (it will shrink during cooking), add the onions, carrot and parsnip and cook, stirring, over medium–high heat until browned. Remove from the pan.

Add the remaining butter to the pan and add the meat, browning well all over. Increase the heat to high and pour in the wine. Bring to the boil, then add the tomato and stock. Return to the boil, then reduce the heat to low, cover and simmer for 2 hours, turning once. Add the vegetables and simmer, covered, for 1 hour.

Remove the meat from the pan and put it on a board ready for carving. Cover with foil and leave it to stand while you finish the sauce. Increase the heat to high and boil the pan juices with the vegetables for 10 minutes to reduce and thicken slightly. Skim off any fat and taste before seasoning. Serve the meat and vegetables with the pan juices. Serve with mustard.

note *Eye of silverside is a tender, long-shaped cut of silverside, which carves easily into serving-sized pieces. A regular piece of silverside or topside may be substituted.*

pork and apple braise

1 tablespoon oil
1 large onion, thinly sliced
1 garlic clove, chopped
2 teaspoons soft brown sugar
2 green apples, cut into wedges
4 pork loin steaks or medallions
2 tablespoons brandy
2 tablespoons seeded mustard
250 ml (9 fl oz/1 cup) chicken stock
140 g (5 oz/²/₃ cup) pitted prunes
125 ml (4 fl oz/½ cup) light cream

serves 4

method Heat the oil in a large heavy-based saucepan. Cook the onion and garlic for 10 minutes over low heat, stirring often, until softened and golden brown. Add the sugar and apple and cook, stirring regularly, until the apple begins to brown. Remove the apple and onion from the pan.

Reheat the pan and lightly brown the pork steaks, two at a time, then return them all to the pan. Add the brandy and stir until it has nearly all evaporated. Add the mustard and stock. Simmer over low heat, covered, for 15 minutes.

Return the apple to the pan with the prunes and cream and simmer for 10 minutes, until the pork is tender. Season to taste before serving.

hint *Take care not to overcook pork or it can become tough and dry.*

linguine with bacon, mushrooms and peas

3 bacon slices
2 teaspoons olive oil
2–3 garlic cloves, crushed
1 red onion, chopped
185 g (7 oz) field mushrooms, sliced
2 large handfuls parsley, chopped
155 g (5 oz/1 cup) peas
375 ml (13 fl oz/1½ cups) low-fat
    evaporated milk
2 teaspoons cornflour (cornstarch)
325 g (11 oz) dried linguine
25 g (1 oz) parmesan cheese shavings
    (optional)

serves 4

method Remove the fat and rind from the bacon and chop roughly. Heat the oil in a medium frying pan, add the garlic, onion and bacon and cook over low heat for 5 minutes, stirring frequently, until the onion and bacon are soft. Add the mushrooms and cook, stirring, for another 5 minutes, or until soft.

Add the parsley, peas and milk to the pan. Mix the cornflour with 1 tablespoon of water until smooth, add to the mixture and stir over medium heat until slightly thickened.

Meanwhile, cook the pasta in a large pan of rapidly boiling, salted water for 8 minutes, or until al dente. Drain and serve with the hot sauce and parmesan shavings, if desired.

beef stroganoff

500 g (1 lb 2 oz) rump steak
cooking oil spray
1 onion, sliced
¼ teaspoon paprika
250 g (9 oz) button mushrooms, halved
2 tablespoons tomato paste
(concentrated purée)
125 ml (4 fl oz/½ cup) beef stock
125 ml (4 fl oz/½ cup) low-fat evaporated milk
3 teaspoons cornflour (cornstarch)
3 tablespoons chopped parsley

serves 4

method Remove any excess fat from the steak and slice into thin strips. Cook in batches in a large, lightly greased non-stick frying pan over high heat, until just cooked. Remove from the pan.

Lightly spray the pan and cook the onion, paprika and mushrooms over medium heat until the onion has softened. Add the meat, tomato paste, stock and 125 ml (4 fl oz/½ cup) water. Bring to the boil, then reduce the heat and simmer for 10 minutes.

In a small bowl, mix the evaporated milk with the cornflour. Add to the pan and stir until the sauce boils and thickens. Sprinkle with parsley.

chicken

rice sticks with chicken and greens

6 baby bok choy (pak choy)

8 stems Chinese broccoli

150 g (5 oz) dried rice stick noodles

2 tablespoons oil

375 g (13 oz) boneless, skinless chicken breasts or tenderloins (underbelly fillets), thinly sliced

2–3 garlic cloves, crushed

5 cm (2 inch) piece fresh ginger, grated

6 spring onions (scallions), cut into short pieces, plus extra, finely shredded spring onion, to garnish

1 tablespoon sherry

90 g (3 oz/1 cup) bean sprouts

sauce

2 teaspoons cornflour (cornstarch)

2 tablespoons soy sauce

2 tablespoons oyster sauce

2 teaspoons soft brown sugar

1 teaspoon sesame oil

serves 4

method   Remove any tough outer leaves from the bok choy and Chinese broccoli. Cut the leaves and stems into bite-sized pieces. Wash well, then drain and dry thoroughly.

Place the rice stick noodles in a large heatproof bowl. Cover with boiling water. Soak for 5–8 minutes, or until softened. Rinse, then drain. Cut into short lengths.

Meanwhile, to make the sauce, mix the cornflour and soy sauce to a smooth paste. Stir in the oyster sauce, brown sugar, sesame oil and 125 ml (4 fl oz/½ cup) water.

Heat the wok until very hot, add the oil and swirl it around to coat the side. Stir-fry the chicken, garlic, ginger and spring onion in batches over high heat for 3–4 minutes, until the chicken is cooked. Remove from the wok.

Add the chopped bok choy, Chinese broccoli and sherry to the wok, cover and steam for 2 minutes, or until wilted. Remove from the wok. Add the sauce to the wok and stir until it is glossy and slightly thickened. Return the chicken, vegetables, noodles and bean sprouts to the wok, and stir until heated through. Serve at once, topped with shredded spring onion.

hint   *Instead of the Chinese broccoli and bok choy, you can use broccoli and English spinach.*

chicken meatballs

500 g (1 lb 2 oz) minced (ground) chicken
3 tablespoons fresh breadcrumbs
2 teaspoons finely chopped thyme
1 tablespoon oil
1 onion, finely chopped
2 x 425 g (15 oz) tins chopped tomatoes
2 teaspoons balsamic vinegar
250 ml (9 fl oz/1 cup) chicken stock
grated parmesan cheese, to serve

serves 6

method   Combine the chicken, breadcrumbs and thyme in a large bowl and season well. Roll tablespoons of the mixture between your hands to make meatballs.

Heat the oil in a large non-stick frying pan and cook the meatballs in batches for 5–8 minutes, or until golden brown. Remove from the pan and drain well on paper towels.

Add the onion to the pan and cook for 2–3 minutes, or until softened. Add the tomato, vinegar and stock, return the meatballs to the pan, then reduce the heat and simmer for 10 minutes, or until the sauce thickens and the meatballs are cooked through. Serve with pasta and a little parmesan.

lemon chilli chicken

2 garlic cloves, chopped
1 tablespoon grated fresh ginger
2 tablespoons olive oil
600 g (1 lb 5 oz) boneless, skinless
   chicken thighs
1 teaspoon ground coriander
2 teaspoons ground cumin
½ teaspoon ground turmeric
1 red chilli, chopped
125 ml (4 fl oz/½ cup) lemon juice
185 ml (6 fl oz/¾ cup) dry white wine
3 large handfuls coriander (cilantro) leaves

serves 4

method   Blend the garlic, ginger and 1 tablespoon water into a paste in a small food processor or with a mortar and pestle. Heat the oil in a heavy-based frying pan and brown the chicken in batches. Remove and set aside.

Add the garlic paste to the pan and cook, stirring, for 1 minute. Add the coriander, cumin, turmeric and chilli and stir-fry for 1 minute more. Stir in the lemon juice and wine.

Add the chicken pieces to the pan. Bring to the boil, reduce the heat, cover and cook for 20–25 minutes, stirring occasionally, until the chicken is tender. Uncover and cook the sauce over high heat for another 5 minutes to reduce it by half. Stir in the fresh coriander and season to taste. Serve with rice.

chicken with peach and ginger salsa

cooking oil spray
4 boneless, skinless chicken breasts
3 tablespoons white wine vinegar
2 tablespoons caster (superfine) sugar
2 teaspoons grated fresh ginger
1 garlic clove, crushed
½ teaspoon ground cumin
1 large handful coriander (cilantro)
leaves, chopped
1 large handful mint, chopped
1 red capsicum (pepper), diced
1 small red onion, finely diced
1 small red chilli, finely chopped
3 peaches, tinned or fresh, diced

serves 4

method Lightly spray a chargrill pan with oil and cook the chicken breasts for 5 minutes on each side or until tender and cooked through.

Combine the vinegar, sugar, ginger, garlic, cumin, coriander and mint. Put the capsicum, onion, chilli and peaches in a bowl. Gently stir through the vinegar mixture and serve at once with the chicken.

chicken and asparagus stir-fry

1 tablespoon oil
1 garlic clove, crushed
10 cm (4 inch) piece fresh ginger, peeled
    and thinly sliced
3 boneless, skinless chicken breasts, sliced
4 spring onions (scallions), sliced
200 g (7 oz) asparagus spears, cut into
    short pieces
2 tablespoons soy sauce
4 tablespoons slivered almonds, roasted

serves 4

method   Heat a wok or large frying pan over high heat, add the oil and swirl to coat. Add the garlic, ginger and chicken and stir-fry for 1–2 minutes, or until the chicken changes colour.

Add the spring onion and asparagus and stir-fry for a further 2 minutes, or until the spring onion is soft.

Stir in the soy sauce and 3 tablespoons water, cover and simmer for 2 minutes, or until the chicken is tender and the vegetables are slightly crisp. Sprinkle with the almonds and serve over steamed rice.

chicken with tomato, olives and capers

2 tablespoons olive oil
1 red onion, cut into thin wedges
1 celery stalk, sliced
150 g (5 oz) cap mushrooms, sliced
3–4 garlic cloves, thinly sliced
8 boneless, skinless chicken thighs
plain (all-purpose) flour, for dusting
125 ml (4 fl oz/½ cup) dry white wine
300 ml (11 fl oz) chicken stock
400 g (14 oz) tin chopped tomatoes
1 tablespoon tomato paste
(concentrated purée)
4 tablespoons black olives
1 tablespoon capers, drained and well rinsed

serves 4

method Heat half the olive oil in a large non-stick frying pan. Add the onion, celery, mushrooms and garlic and cook, stirring, for 5 minutes, or until the onion is soft. Remove from the pan.

Coat the chicken lightly in flour, shaking off any excess. Heat the remaining oil in the frying pan and cook the chicken, in batches, turning once, for 5 minutes, or until well browned. Add the white wine and stock and cook for a further 2 minutes.

Return the vegetables to the pan and add the tomato and tomato paste. Simmer, partially covered, for 40 minutes, or until thickened. Add the olives and capers and season.

curried chicken in spicy tomato sauce

1 tablespoon olive oil
2 x 1.5 kg (3 lb 5 oz) chickens, jointed
1 onion, sliced
½ teaspoon ground cloves
1 teaspoon ground turmeric
2 teaspoons garam masala
3 teaspoons chilli powder
3 garlic cloves
1 tablespoon finely chopped fresh ginger
1 tablespoon poppy seeds
2 teaspoons fennel seeds
3 cardamom pods, seeds removed
  (see Note)
250 ml (9 fl oz/1 cup) light coconut milk
1 star anise
1 cinnamon stick
4 large tomatoes, roughly chopped
2 tablespoons lime juice

serves 10

method   Heat the oil in a large frying pan, add the chicken in batches and cook for 5–10 minutes, or until browned, then transfer to a large saucepan.

Add the onion to the frying pan and cook, stirring, for 10–12 minutes, or until golden. Stir in the cloves, turmeric, garam masala and chilli powder, and cook, stirring, for 1 minute, then add to the chicken.

Place the garlic, ginger, poppy seeds, fennel seeds, cardamom seeds and 2 tablespoons of the coconut milk in a food processor or blender, and process until smooth. Add the spice mixture, the remaining coconut milk, star anise, cinnamon, tomato and 3 tablespoons water to the chicken. Simmer, covered, for 45 minutes, or until the chicken is tender. Remove the chicken, cover and keep warm.

Bring the cooking liquid to the boil and boil for 20–25 minutes, or until reduced by half. Mix the lime juice with the cooking liquid and pour over the chicken. Serve with low-fat yoghurt.

note   *To remove the cardamom seeds from the cardamom pods, crush the pods with the flat side of a heavy knife, then peel away the pod with your fingers, scraping out the seeds.*

steamed lemongrass and ginger chicken

200 g (7 oz) fresh egg noodles
4 boneless, skinless chicken breasts
2 lemongrass stems
5 cm (2 inch) piece fresh ginger,
cut into thin strips
1 lime, thinly sliced
500 ml (17 fl oz/2 cups) chicken stock
350 g (12 oz/1 bunch) choy sum, cut into
10 cm (4 inch) lengths
800 g (1 lb 12 oz) Chinese broccoli, cut into
10 cm (4 inch) lengths
3 tablespoons kecap manis
(see Note, page 8)
3 tablespoons soy sauce
1 teaspoon sesame oil
toasted sesame seeds, to garnish

serves 4

method Cook the noodles in a saucepan of boiling water for 5 minutes. Drain and keep warm.

Cut each chicken breast fillet horizontally through the middle so that you are left with eight thin flat chicken fillets. Cut the lemongrass into lengths about 5 cm (2 inches) longer than the chicken breasts, then cut in half lengthways. Place one piece of lemongrass onto one half of each chicken breast, top with some ginger and lime slices, then top with the other half of the breast.

Pour the stock into a wok and bring to a simmer. Place two of the chicken breasts in a paper-lined bamboo steamer. Put the steamer over the wok and steam over the simmering stock for 12–15 minutes, or until the chicken is tender. Remove from the steamer, cover and keep warm. Repeat with the rest of the chicken.

Steam the greens in the same way for 3 minutes, or until tender. Bring the stock in the wok to the boil.

Place the kecap manis, soy sauce and sesame oil in a bowl and whisk together well. Divide the noodles among four serving plates and ladle the boiling stock over them. Top with a pile of Asian greens, then add the chicken and generously drizzle each serve with the sauce. Sprinkle with toasted sesame seeds and serve.

asian barbecued chicken

2 garlic cloves, finely chopped
3 tablespoons hoisin sauce
3 teaspoons light soy sauce
3 teaspoons honey
1 teaspoon sesame oil
2 tablespoons tomato sauce (ketchup)
    or sweet chilli sauce
2 spring onions (scallions), finely sliced
1.5 kg (3 lb 5 oz) chicken wings

serves 6

method To make the marinade, combine the garlic, hoisin sauce, soy sauce, honey, sesame oil, tomato sauce and spring onion in a small bowl. Pour over the chicken wings, cover and marinate in the refrigerator for at least 2 hours.

Cook the chicken in batches on a barbecue grill plate or flat plate, turning once, for 20–25 minutes, or until cooked and golden brown. Baste with the marinade during cooking. Heat any remaining marinade in a saucepan until boiling and serve as a sauce.

note *The chicken can also be baked in a 180°C (350°F/Gas 4) oven for 30 minutes (turn once).*

lemongrass chicken skewers

4 boneless, skinless chicken thighs
1½ tablespoons soft brown sugar
1½ tablespoons lime juice
2 teaspoons green curry paste
18 makrut (kaffir lime) leaves
2 lemongrass stems

mango salsa

1 small mango, finely diced
1 teaspoon grated lime zest
2 teaspoons lime juice
1 teaspoon soft brown sugar
½ teaspoon fish sauce

serves 4

method Cut the fat from the chicken and then cut the fillets in half lengthways. Combine the brown sugar, lime juice, curry paste and two of the makrut leaves, shredded, in a bowl. Add the chicken and mix well. Cover and refrigerate overnight, or for several hours.

Trim the lemongrass to measure about 20 cm (8 inches), leaving the root end intact, then cut lengthways into four pieces. Cut a slit in each of the remaining makrut leaves and thread one onto each skewer. Cut two slits in the chicken and thread onto the lemongrass, followed by another makrut leaf. Repeat with the remaining makrut leaves, chicken and lemongrass. Pan-fry or barbecue until cooked through.

To make the salsa, put all the ingredients in a bowl and stir gently to combine. Serve with the chicken.

orange and rosemary glazed chicken

2 seedless oranges
175 g (6 oz/½ cup) honey
2 tablespoons dijon mustard
1½ tablespoons chopped rosemary
4 garlic cloves, crushed
1.5 kg (3 lb 5 oz) chicken pieces

serves 6

method   Squeeze the juice from one orange into a bowl, add the honey, dijon mustard, rosemary and garlic and mix together well. Cut the other orange in half and then cut it into slices.

Add the chicken and orange slices to the orange juice mixture. Season and mix well and marinate for at least 4 hours.

Preheat the oven to 200°C (400°F/Gas 6). Line a large roasting tin with foil. Arrange the chicken and the marinade in the roasting tin. Bake for 40–50 minutes, or until the chicken is golden, turning once and basting with the marinade.

chicken with black bean sauce

2 tablespoons black beans
1 tablespoon oil
1 small onion, finely chopped
1 tablespoon finely chopped fresh ginger
1 garlic clove, finely chopped
1 red chilli, seeded and finely chopped
310 ml (11 fl oz/1¼ cups) chicken stock
2 teaspoons cornflour (cornstarch)
2 teaspoons sesame oil
4 boneless, skinless chicken breasts

serves 4

method   Rinse the black beans under cold water for 3–4 minutes to remove any excess saltiness. Drain well.

Heat the oil in a small saucepan and add the onion, ginger, garlic and chilli. Cook over low heat until the onion is soft but not browned. Add the chicken stock and bring to the boil. Reduce the heat and simmer for 5 minutes.

Mix the cornflour and 1 tablespoon water in a small bowl and add to the pan. Keep stirring and the mixture will thicken. Allow to simmer for 3 minutes, then add the black beans and sesame oil and mix together well.

Grill (broil) the chicken under a preheated grill (broiler) for 5 minutes on each side, or until cooked through and tender. Serve with the sauce.

note   *Black beans are available tinned or in vacuum packs from Asian food stores. Do not confuse these Chinese black beans with Mexican black turtle beans that are available from health food shops. The two varieties are very different.*

baked chicken and leek risotto

1 tablespoon oil
1 leek, white part only, thinly sliced
2 boneless, skinless chicken breasts, cubed
440 g (15 oz/2 cups) arborio rice
3 tablespoons dry white wine
1.25 litres (44 fl oz/5 cups) chicken stock
4 tablespoons grated parmesan cheese
2 tablespoons thyme leaves
thyme leaves and parmesan cheese,
    for serving

serves 6

method Preheat the oven to 150°C (300°F/Gas 2) and place a 5 litre (20 cup) ovenproof dish with a lid in the oven to warm. Heat the oil in a saucepan over medium heat, add the leek and cook for 2 minutes, or until soft.

Add the chicken and cook, stirring, for 2–3 minutes, or until it colours. Add the rice and stir so that it is well coated. Cook for 1 minute.

Add the wine and chicken stock and bring to the boil. Pour the mixture into the warm ovenproof dish. Bake, covered, for 30 minutes, stirring halfway through. Remove from the oven and stir in the parmesan and thyme leaves. Season to taste. Sprinkle with extra thyme leaves and a little parmesan and serve.

tandoori chicken

125 g (5 oz/½ cup) Greek-style low-fat
natural yoghurt
2 tablespoons tandoori paste
2 garlic cloves, crushed
2 tablespoons lime juice
1½ teaspoons garam masala
2 tablespoons finely chopped coriander
(cilantro) leaves
6 boneless, skinless chicken thighs,
fat removed

serves 4

method   Combine the yoghurt, tandoori paste, garlic, lime juice, garam masala and coriander in a bowl and mix well. Add the chicken, coat well, cover and refrigerate for at least 1 hour.

Preheat a barbecue grill plate or flat plate and sightly brush with oil. Cook the chicken, in batches if necessary, for 10–15 minutes on medium heat, turning once and basting with the remaining marinade until golden and cooked through. Serve with cucumber raita and naan bread.

spicy chicken patties

500 g (1 lb 2 oz) minced (ground) chicken
4 spring onions (scallions), finely chopped
2 large handfuls coriander (cilantro) leaves, finely chopped
2 garlic cloves, crushed
¾ teaspoon cayenne pepper
1 egg white, lightly beaten
1 tablespoon oil
1 lemon, halved

serves 4

method Preheat the oven to 170°C (325°F/Gas 3). Mix together all the ingredients except the oil and lemon, season with salt and pepper and shape the mixture into 4 patties. Refrigerate for 20 minutes before cooking.

Heat the oil in a large frying pan over medium heat, add the patties and cook for about 5 minutes on each side, or until browned and cooked through.

Squeeze the lemon on the cooked patties and drain well on paper towels. Serve with a salad or use to make burgers with crusty rolls.

chicken with tomato and mango chutney

8 chicken drumsticks, scored
1 tablespoon mustard powder
2 tablespoons tomato sauce (ketchup)
1 tablespoon sweet mango chutney
1 teaspoon worcestershire sauce
1 tablespoon dijon mustard
3 tablespoons raisins
1 tablespoon oil

serves 4

method Toss the chicken in the mustard powder and season. Combine the tomato sauce, chutney, worcestershire sauce, mustard, raisins and oil. Spoon over the chicken and toss well to coat evenly. Marinate for 2 hours, or overnight, turning once.

Preheat the oven to 200°C (400°F/Gas 6). Put the chicken in a shallow roasting tin and bake for 45 minutes, or until the meat comes away from the bone.

hint *Serve with toasted Turkish bread and a mixture of yoghurt, cucumber and mint.*

lime steamed chicken

2 limes, thinly sliced
4 boneless, skinless chicken breasts
500 g (1 lb 2 oz/1 bunch) bok choy (pak choy)
500 g (1 lb 2 oz/1 bunch) choy sum
1 teaspoon sesame oil
1 tablespoon peanut oil
125 ml (4 fl oz/½ cup) oyster sauce
4 tablespoons lime juice

serves 4

method   Line the base of a bamboo steamer with the lime, place the chicken on top and season. Place over a wok with a little water in the base, cover and steam for 8–10 minutes, or until the chicken is cooked through. Cover the chicken and keep warm. Remove the water from the wok.

Wash and trim the greens. Heat the oils in the wok and cook the greens for 2–3 minutes, or until they are just wilted.

Combine the oyster sauce and lime juice and pour over the greens when they are cooked. Place the chicken on serving plates on top of the greens and serve with rice, and lime slices.

note   *The Asian green vegetables used in this recipe, bok choy and choy sum, can be replaced by any green vegetables, such as broccoli, snow peas (mangetouts) or English spinach.*

chicken with oyster sauce and basil

3 tablespoons oyster sauce
2 tablespoons fish sauce
1 tablespoon grated palm sugar (jaggery)
1 tablespoon oil
2–3 garlic cloves, crushed
1 tablespoon grated fresh ginger
1–2 red chillies, seeded and finely chopped
4 spring onions (scallions), finely chopped
375 g (13 oz) boneless, skinless chicken breasts,
cut into thin strips
250 g (9 oz) broccoli, cut into florets
230 g (8 oz) tin water chestnuts, drained
230 g (8 oz) tin sliced bamboo shoots, rinsed
20 basil leaves, shredded

serves 4

method   Put 3 tablespoons water in a small bowl with the oyster sauce, fish sauce and palm sugar. Mix well.

Heat the wok until very hot, add the oil and swirl it around to coat the side. Stir-fry the garlic, ginger, chilli and spring onion for 1 minute over medium heat. Increase the heat to medium–high, add the chicken and stir-fry for 2–3 minutes, or until it is just cooked. Remove from the wok.

Reheat the wok and add the broccoli, water chestnuts and bamboo shoots. Stir-fry for 2–3 minutes, tossing constantly. Add the sauce and bring to the boil, tossing constantly. Return the chicken to the wok and toss until it is heated through. Stir in the basil and serve at once.

seafood

chargrilled baby octopus

1 kg (2 lb 4 oz) baby octopus
185 ml (6 fl oz/¾ cup) red wine
2 tablespoons balsamic vinegar
2 tablespoons soy sauce
2 tablespoons hoisin sauce
1 garlic clove, crushed
cooking oil spray

serves 4

method   Cut off the octopus heads below the eyes with a sharp knife. Discard the heads and guts. Push the beaks out with your index finger, remove and discard. Wash the octopus thoroughly under running water and drain on paper towels. If the octopus are large, cut the tentacles into quarters.

Put the octopus in a large bowl. Stir together the wine, vinegar, soy sauce, hoisin sauce and garlic in a bowl and pour over the octopus. Toss to coat, cover and refrigerate for several hours, or overnight.

Heat a chargrill pan or barbecue grill plate or flat plate until very hot and then lightly oil. Drain the octopus, reserving the marinade. Cook in batches for 3–5 minutes, until the octopus flesh turns white. Brush the marinade over the octopus during cooking. Be careful not to overcook or the octopus will be tough. Serve warm or cold. Delicious with a green salad and lime wedges.

tuna with coriander noodles

3 tablespoons lime juice
2 tablespoons fish sauce
2 tablespoons sweet chilli sauce
2 teaspoons grated palm sugar (jaggery)
1 teaspoon sesame oil
1 garlic clove, finely chopped
1 tablespoon virgin olive oil
4 tuna steaks
200 g (7 oz) dried thin wheat noodles
6 spring onions (scallions), thinly sliced
2 large handfuls coriander (cilantro) leaves,
chopped, plus extra, to garnish

serves 4

method   To make the dressing, place the lime juice, fish sauce, chilli sauce, sugar, sesame oil and garlic in a small bowl and mix together.

Heat the olive oil in a chargrill pan. Add the tuna steaks and cook over high heat for 2 minutes on each side, or until cooked to your liking. Transfer the steaks to a warm plate, cover and keep warm.

Put the noodles in a large saucepan of lightly salted, rapidly boiling water and return to the boil. Cook for 4 minutes, or until tender. Drain well. Add half the dressing and half the spring onion and coriander to the noodles and gently toss together.

Either cut the tuna into even cubes or slice it. Place the noodles on serving plates and top with the tuna. Mix the remaining dressing with the spring onion and coriander and drizzle over the tuna. Garnish with coriander leaves.

prawns with jasmine rice

1 tablespoon peanut oil
8 spring onions (scallions), sliced
1 tablespoon finely chopped fresh ginger
1 tablespoon finely sliced lemongrass, white
    part only
2 teaspoons crushed coriander seeds
    (see Note)
400 g (14 oz/2 cups) jasmine rice
1 litre (35 fl oz/4 cups) vegetable stock
1 tablespoon shredded lime zest
1 kg (2 lb 4 oz) raw prawns (shrimp), peeled,
    deveined and chopped
2 tablespoons lime juice
2 very large handfuls coriander (cilantro) leaves
fish sauce, for serving

serves 4

method Heat the oil in a saucepan, add the spring onion and cook over low heat for 4 minutes, or until soft. Add the ginger, lemongrass, coriander seeds and rice, and stir for 1 minute.

Add the stock and lime zest and bring to the boil while stirring. Reduce the heat to very low and cook, covered, for 15–20 minutes, or until the rice is tender.

Remove the pan from the heat and stir in the prawns. Cover and set aside for 4–5 minutes, or until the prawns are cooked. Add the lime juice and coriander leaves and fluff the rice with a fork. Sprinkle with a few drops of fish sauce to serve.

note *To crush coriander seeds, place in a small plastic bag and, using a rolling pin, crush until fine.*

clams in roasted chilli paste

roasted chilli paste

2 tablespoons oil
2 spring onions (scallions), sliced
2 garlic cloves, sliced
3 tablespoons small dried shrimp
6 small red chillies, seeded
2 teaspoons palm sugar (jaggery)
2 teaspoons fish sauce
2 teaspoons tamarind concentrate

3 garlic cloves, finely sliced
3 small red chillies, seeded and
sliced lengthways
1 tablespoon light soy sauce
250 ml (9 fl oz/1 cup) chicken stock
1 kg (2 lb 4 oz) clams (vongole), scrubbed
1 large handful Thai basil leaves

serves 4

method To make the roasted chilli paste, heat the oil in a wok and fry the spring onion, garlic, dried shrimp and chillies until golden brown. Remove with a slotted spoon and keep the oil.

Put the onion, garlic, shrimp, chillies and sugar in a mortar and pestle or small food processor and grind until the mixture is well blended. Add the fish sauce, tamarind concentrate and a pinch of salt. Blend or grind to a fine paste. Transfer to a bowl.

Heat the reserved oil in the wok. Add the garlic, chilli, roasted chilli paste and soy sauce. Mix well, add the stock and bring just to the boil. Add the clams and cook over medium–high heat for 2–3 minutes. Discard any unopened clams. Stir in the basil and serve immediately with steamed jasmine rice.

thai-style whole snapper

2 garlic cloves, crushed
1 tablespoon fish sauce
2 tablespoons lemon juice
1 tablespoon grated fresh ginger
2 tablespoons sweet chilli sauce
2 tablespoons chopped coriander (cilantro)
1 tablespoon rice wine vinegar
2 tablespoons dry white wine
600 g (1 lb 5 oz) whole snapper, cleaned and
    scaled (ask your fishmonger to do this)
2 spring onions (scallions), cut into thin strips

serves 6

method   Preheat the oven to 190°C (375°F/Gas 5). Place the garlic, fish sauce, lemon juice, ginger, chilli sauce, coriander, vinegar and wine in a bowl and mix together well.

Place the snapper on a large piece of foil on a baking tray. Pour the marinade over the fish and sprinkle with the spring onion.

Wrap the foil around the fish like a parcel and place in the oven. Bake for 20–30 minutes or until the flesh flakes easily when tested with a fork. Serve immediately with steamed rice.

fusilli with tuna, capers and parsley

425 g (15 oz) can tuna in spring water, drained
2 tablespoons olive oil
2 garlic cloves, finely chopped
2 small red chillies, finely chopped
3 tablespoons capers, drained and
well rinsed (see Note)
2 very large handfuls parsley, finely chopped
3 tablespoons lemon juice
375 g (13 oz) fusilli

serves 4

method   Place the tuna in a bowl and flake lightly with a fork. Combine the olive oil, garlic, chilli, capers, parsley and lemon juice. Pour over the tuna and mix lightly. Season well.

Meanwhile, cook the pasta in a large saucepan of rapidly boiling salted water until al dente. Reserve 125 ml (4 fl oz/1/2 cup) of the cooking water, then drain the pasta. Toss the tuna mixture through the pasta, adding enough of the reserved water to give a moist consistency. Serve immediately.

note   *Generally, the smaller the caper the tastier, so use baby ones if you can find them.*

japanese-style salmon parcels

2 teaspoons sesame seeds
4 x 150 g (5 oz) salmon cutlets or steaks
2.5 cm (1 inch) piece fresh ginger
2 celery stalks
4 spring onions (scallions)
¼ teaspoon dashi granules
3 tablespoons mirin
2 tablespoons tamari

serves 4

method   Cut four squares of baking paper large enough to enclose the salmon steaks. Preheat the oven to 230°C (450°F/Gas 8). Lightly toast the sesame seeds under a hot grill (broiler) for 1 minute.

Wash the salmon and dry with paper towels. Place a salmon cutlet in the centre of each baking paper square. Cut the ginger into paper-thin slices. Slice the celery and spring onions into short lengths, then lengthways into fine strips. Arrange a bundle of celery and spring onion and several slices of ginger on each salmon steak.

Combine the dashi granules, mirin and tamari in a small saucepan. Heat gently until the dashi granules dissolve. Drizzle over each parcel, sprinkle with sesame seeds and carefully wrap the salmon, folding in the sides to seal in all the juices. Arrange the parcels on a baking tray and cook for about 12 minutes, or until tender. (The paper will puff up when the fish is cooked.) Do not overcook or the salmon will dry out. Serve immediately, as standing time can spoil the fish.

note   *Dashi, mirin and tamari are all available from Asian food stores.*

calamari with spicy sauce

500 g (l lb 2 oz) squid tubes, cleaned
2 lemongrass stems, white part only,
finely chopped
3 teaspoons grated fresh ginger
3 garlic cloves, finely chopped
½ teaspoon chopped red chilli
1 tablespoon oil
2 very ripe tomatoes
150 g (5 oz) mixed lettuce
1 handful coriander (cilantro) leaves
2 tablespoons lime juice
1 teaspoon finely grated lime zest
1 red capsicum (pepper), cut into strips

lime, chilli and garlic sauce

3 tablespoons lime juice
1 tablespoon lemon juice
2 tablespoons fish sauce
1 tablespoon caster (superfine) sugar
2 teaspoons chopped red chilli
2 garlic cloves, finely chopped
1 tablespoon finely chopped coriander
(cilantro)

serves 4

method   Cut the squid tubes open, wash and pat dry. Cut shallow slashes about 5 mm (¼ inch) apart on the soft inside, in a diamond pattern, then cut into 3 cm (1¼ inch) strips. Mix in a bowl with the lemongrass, ginger, garlic, chilli and oil. Cover with plastic wrap and refrigerate for 3 hours.

Cut the tomatoes in half, scoop out the membrane and seeds and finely chop them, retaining the juices. Cut the flesh into small cubes and set aside. Arrange the lettuce and coriander leaves in serving bowls.

Just before serving, lightly grease and heat a barbecue grill plate or flat plate or large, heavy non-stick frying pan until very hot. Quickly cook the squid in batches, tossing for 2–3 minutes, until just tender and curled, sprinkling the lime juice and zest over the top. Remove the squid, toss with the chopped tomato seeds and arrange on the salad. Scatter the tomato and capsicum over the top. Season well. Stir the sauce ingredients together until the sugar dissolves. Drizzle over the squid.

sardines with capsicum and eggplant

2 large red capsicums (peppers), quartered
   and seeded
4 long thin eggplants (aubergines), cut
   into quarters lengthways
cooking oil spray
16 fresh sardines, butterflied
   (about 300 g/11 oz)
1 slice white bread, crusts removed
1 handful parsley
1 garlic clove, crushed
1 teaspoon grated lemon zest

dressing

1 tablespoon olive oil
1 tablespoon balsamic vinegar
½ teaspoon soft brown sugar
1 garlic clove, crushed
1 tablespoon snipped fresh chives

serves 4

method   Preheat the oven to 180°C (350°F/Gas 4). Lightly grease a large baking dish with oil. Preheat the grill (broiler) and line with foil.

Grill (broil) the capsicum until the skin is blistered and blackened. Cool in a plastic bag for 10 minutes, peel away the skin and slice thickly lengthways. Lightly spray the eggplant with oil and grill each side for 3–5 minutes, until softened.

Combine the dressing ingredients in a screw-top jar and shake well. Put the capsicum and eggplant in a bowl, pour the dressing over, toss well and set aside.

Place the sardines on a baking tray in a single layer, well spaced. Finely chop the bread, parsley, garlic and lemon zest together in a food processor. Sprinkle over each sardine. Bake for 10–15 minutes, until cooked through. Serve with the capsicum and eggplant.

mussels in chunky tomato sauce

1.5 kg (3 lb 5 oz) black mussels
1 tablespoon olive oil
1 large onion, diced
4 garlic cloves, finely chopped
2 x 400 g (14 oz) tins chopped tomatoes
3 tablespoons tomato paste
(concentrated purée)
3 tablespoons pitted black olives
1 tablespoon capers, drained and well rinsed
125 ml (4 fl oz/½ cup) fish stock
3 tablespoons chopped parsley

serves 6

method   Scrub the mussels with a stiff brush and pull out the hairy beards. Discard any broken mussels, or open ones that don't close when tapped on the work surface. Rinse well.

In a large saucepan, heat the olive oil and cook the onion and garlic over medium heat for 1–2 minutes, until softened. Add the tomato, tomato paste, olives, capers and fish stock. Bring to the boil, then reduce the heat and simmer, stirring occasionally, for 20 minutes, or until the sauce is thick.

Stir in the mussels and cover the pan. Shake or toss the mussels occasionally and cook for 4–5 minutes, or until the mussels begin to open. Remove the pan from the heat and discard any mussels that haven't opened in the cooking time. Just before serving, toss the parsley through.

tuna kebabs

1 tablespoon olive oil
2–3 small red chillies, seeded and
    finely chopped
3–4 garlic cloves, crushed
1 red onion, finely chopped
3 tomatoes, seeded and chopped
3 tablespoons dry white wine or water
2 x 300 g (11 oz) tins chickpeas, drained
    and rinsed
1 small handful oregano, chopped
1 very large handful parsley, chopped
1 kg (2 lb 4 oz) tuna fillet, cut into 4 cm
    (1½ inch) cubes
8 rosemary stalks, about 20 cm (8 inches) long,
    with leaves
cooking oil spray
lemon wedges, to serve

serves 4

method   Heat the oil in a large frying pan, add the chilli, garlic and red onion and stir for 5 minutes, or until softened. Add the tomato and wine or water. Cook over low heat for 10 minutes, or until the mixture is soft, pulpy and the liquid has evaporated. Stir in the chickpeas, oregano and parsley. Season with salt and pepper.

Heat a barbeque grill plate or flat plate. Thread the tuna onto the rosemary stalks, lightly spray with oil, then cook, turning, for 3 minutes. Do not overcook or the tuna will fall apart. Serve with the chickpeas and lemon.

cod with papaya and black bean salsa

1 small red onion, finely chopped
1 papaya (about 500 g/1 lb 2 oz), peeled, seeded and cubed
1 bird's-eye chilli (pepper), seeded and finely chopped
1 tablespoon salted black beans, drained and rinsed
cooking oil spray
4 blue-eyed cod cutlets
2 teaspoons peanut oil
1 teaspoon sesame oil
2 teaspoons fish sauce
1 tablespoon lime juice
1 tablespoon chopped fresh coriander (cilantro) leaves
2 teaspoons shredded fresh mint

serves 4

method   Toss together the onion, papaya, chilli and black beans.

Heat a chargrill pan or plate and lightly spray with oil. Add the cod and cook for 2 minutes each side, or until cooked to your liking.

Whisk together the peanut oil, sesame oil, fish sauce and lime juice. Pour over the papaya and black bean salsa and toss. Add the coriander and mint and serve immediately, at room temperature, with the fish.

note   *Black beans have a distinctive taste, so if you are not familiar with them, taste them before adding to the salsa. If you prefer not to add them, the salsa is equally delicious without. Pawpaw can be used instead of papaya. It is a larger fruit from the same family, with yellower flesh and a less sweet flavour.*

crumbed fish with wasabi cream

60 g (2 oz/¾ cup) fresh breadcrumbs
25 g (1 oz/¾ cup) cornflakes
1 sheet nori (dried seaweed), torn roughly
   (see Note)
¼ teaspoon paprika
4 x 150 g (5 oz) pieces firm white fish fillets
plain (all-purpose) flour, for dusting
1 egg white
1 tablespoon skim milk
1 spring onion (scallion), thinly sliced

wasabi cream

125 g (5 oz/½ cup) low-fat natural yoghurt
1 teaspoon wasabi (see Note)
1 tablespoon low-fat mayonnaise
1 teaspoon lime juice

serves 4

method   Preheat the oven to 180°C (350°F/Gas 4). Combine the breadcrumbs, cornflakes, nori and paprika in a food processor and process until the nori is finely chopped.

Dust the fish lightly with the flour, dip into the combined egg white and milk, then into the breadcrumb mixture. Press the crumb mixture onto the fish firmly, then refrigerate for 15 minutes.

Line a baking tray with baking paper and put the fish on the paper. Bake for 15–20 minutes, or until the fish flakes easily with a fork.

To make the wasabi cream, mix the ingredients thoroughly in a bowl. Serve with the fish and sprinkle with a little spring onion.

note   *Wasabi paste (a pungent paste, also known as Japanese horseradish) and nori (sheets of paper-thin dried seaweed) are both available from Asian food stores.*

swordfish with pineapple salsa

375 g (13 oz/2 cups) diced pineapple
1 small red onion, chopped
1 red capsicum (pepper), chopped
1 jalapeño chilli, seeded
1 tablespoon grated fresh ginger
finely grated zest of 1 lime
1 tablespoon lime juice
1 large handful coriander (cilantro) leaves,
chopped
4 swordfish steaks

serves 4

method   Put the pineapple, onion, capsicum, chilli and ginger in a food processor and process in short bursts until coarsely chopped. Stir in the lime zest and juice and the coriander leaves. Season with salt and pour into a small bowl. Cover and leave the salsa for 2 hours.

Meanwhile, soak four wooden skewers in cold water for 30 minutes to prevent scorching. Drain off any excess liquid from the salsa.

Cut the swordfish into cubes and thread onto the skewers. Grill under a hot grill (broiler) for 3 minutes on each side, or until cooked through. Serve the skewers with the salsa.

crab, chilli and coriander noodles

1 tablespoon oil
4 spring onions (scallions), finely sliced
3 garlic cloves, crushed
2 green chillies, seeded and finely sliced
400 g (14 oz) fresh crabmeat
3 tablespoons lime juice
3 teaspoons grated lime zest
1 teaspoon caster (superfine) sugar
2 teaspoons sambal oelek (South-East Asian chilli paste)
375 g (13 oz) thin dried egg noodles
1 teaspoon sesame oil
2 tablespoons sweet chilli sauce
4 tablespoons chopped coriander (cilantro)

serves 4

method   Heat the oil in a large frying pan and add the spring onion, garlic and green chilli. Cook for 1–2 minutes over low heat, until soft. Add the crabmeat, lime juice and zest, caster sugar and sambal oelek. Stir until heated through and season to taste with salt.

Cook the noodles in a large saucepan of boiling salted water for 2–3 minutes, or until tender. Drain well and toss with the sesame oil. Add the crab mixture, sweet chilli sauce and coriander to the noodles and gently toss. Serve immediately.

note   *You can also use tinned crabmeat instead of fresh, but you will need 4 x 200 g (7 oz) tins, as a lot of weight will be lost when the meat is drained.*

tuna with lime and chilli sauce

2 large handfuls mint leaves, chopped
2 large handfuls coriander (cilantro) leaves, chopped, plus extra, to garnish
1 teaspoon grated lime zest
1 tablespoon lime juice
1 teaspoon grated fresh ginger
1 jalapeño chilli (pepper), seeded and finely chopped
250 g (9 oz/1 cup) low-fat natural yoghurt
4 tuna steaks

serves 4

method Mix together the mint, coriander, lime zest, lime juice, ginger and chilli. Fold in the yoghurt and season with salt and freshly ground black pepper.

Cook the tuna in a lightly oiled chargrill pan for 2 minutes on each side. Serve the tuna with the sauce and garnish with coriander leaves.

note *Jalapeño chillies are smooth and thick-fleshed and are available as both red and green. They are quite fiery and you can use a less powerful variety of chilli if you prefer.*

steamed trout with ginger and coriander

2 whole rainbow trout (about 320 g/
    11 oz each), cleaned and scaled
2 limes, thinly sliced
5 cm (2 inch) piece fresh ginger, cut into
    matchsticks
3 tablespoons caster (superfine) sugar
3 tablespoons lime juice
zest of 1 lime, cut into thin strips
1 large handful coriander (cilantro) leaves

serves 2

method   Preheat the oven to 180°C (350°F/Gas 4). Fill the fish cavities with the lime slices and some of the ginger, then place the fish on a large piece of greased foil. Wrap the fish and bake on a baking tray for 20–30 minutes, until the flesh flakes easily when tested with a fork.

Meanwhile, combine the sugar and lime juice with 250 ml (9 fl oz/1 cup) water in a small saucepan and stir without boiling until the sugar dissolves. Bring to the boil, then reduce the heat and simmer for 10 minutes, or until syrupy. Stir in the remaining ginger and lime zest. Put the fish on a plate. Top with coriander leaves and pour the hot syrup over it.

spaghetti marinara

2 teaspoons olive oil
1 onion, chopped
2 garlic cloves, crushed
125 ml (4 fl oz/½ cup) dry red wine
2 tablespoons tomato paste
(concentrated purée)
425 g (15 oz) tin chopped tomatoes
250 ml (9 fl oz/1 cup) bottled tomato
pasta sauce
1 tablespoon chopped basil
1 tablespoon chopped oregano
12 mussels, hairy beards removed,
and scrubbed
30 g (1 oz) butter
125 g (5 oz) small squid tubes, cleaned
and sliced
125 g (5 oz) boneless firm white fish
fillets, cubed
200 g (7 oz) raw prawns (shrimp), peeled and
deveined, tails intact
500 g (1 lb 2 oz) spaghetti

serves 4

method   Heat the oil in a large pan and cook the onion and garlic over low heat for 2–3 minutes. Increase the heat to medium and add the wine, tomato paste, tomato and pasta sauce. Simmer, stirring occasionally, for 5–10 minutes or until the sauce reduces and thickens slightly. Stir in the herbs and season to taste. Keep warm.

While the sauce is simmering, heat 125 ml (4 fl oz/½ cup) water in a saucepan. Discard any broken mussels, or open ones that don't close when tapped on the work surface. Rinse well. Add the mussels. Cover and steam for 3–5 minutes, or until the mussels have opened and changed colour. Remove from the pan. Discard any unopened mussels. Stir the liquid into the tomato sauce.

Heat the butter in a frying pan and sauté the squid, fish and prawns, in batches, for 1–2 minutes, until cooked. Add the seafood to the warm tomato sauce and stir gently.

Cook the pasta in a large saucepan of rapidly boiling salted water until al dente and then drain. Toss the seafood sauce with the pasta.

vegetarian

chargrilled vegetable terrine

350 g (12 oz) ricotta cheese

2 garlic cloves, crushed

8 large slices chargrilled eggplant (aubergine), drained (see Note)

10 slices chargrilled red capsicum (pepper), drained

8 slices chargrilled zucchini (courgette), drained

100 g (4 oz) marinated mushrooms, drained and halved

45 g (1½ oz) rocket (arugula) leaves

3 marinated artichokes, drained and sliced

85 g (3 oz) semi-dried (sun-blushed) tomatoes, drained and chopped

serves 8

method Line a 24 x 13 x 6 cm (9½ x 5 x 2½ inch) loaf tin with plastic wrap, leaving a generous amount hanging over the sides. Place the ricotta and garlic in a bowl and beat until smooth. Season with salt and pepper to taste and set aside.

Line the base of the tin with half the eggplant, cutting and fitting to cover the base. Top with a layer of half the capsicum, then all the zucchini. Spread with the ricotta mixture and press down firmly. Top with a layer of half the mushrooms. Place the rocket leaves on top of the mushrooms. Arrange the artichoke, tomato and remaining mushrooms in three rows lengthways on top of the rocket.

Top with another layer of capsicum and finish with the eggplant. Fold the overhanging plastic wrap over the top of the terrine. Put a piece of cardboard on top and weigh it down with weights or small food tins. Refrigerate the terrine overnight.

To serve, peel back the plastic wrap and turn the terrine out onto a plate. Remove the plastic wrap and cut the terrine into thick slices.

note *You can buy chargrilled eggplant, capsicum and zucchini, and marinated mushrooms and artichokes at delicatessens.*

vegetable strudel parcels

300 g (11 oz) pumpkin (winter squash)
2 carrots
1 parsnip
2 celery stalks
2 teaspoons sesame oil
1 onion, finely sliced
3 teaspoons finely chopped or
grated fresh ginger
1 tablespoon dry sherry
1 teaspoon finely grated lemon zest
185 g (7 oz/1 cup) cooked long-grain rice
2 tablespoons plum sauce
1 tablespoon sweet chilli sauce
2 teaspoons soy sauce
16 sheets filo pastry
4 tablespoons dry breadcrumbs
1 teaspoon butter, melted
1 tablespoon sesame seeds
sweet chilli sauce, for serving

serves 4

method   Cut the pumpkin, carrots, parsnip and celery into thick matchsticks 3 mm (1/8 inch) wide and 5 cm (2 inches) long. Heat the oil in a wok over medium heat and stir-fry the onion and ginger until brown. Add the pumpkin, carrot and parsnip, toss and cook for 1 minute. Sprinkle 2 teaspoons water over the vegetables, cover and steam for 1 minute. Add the celery, sherry and lemon zest, toss and cook for 1 minute. Cover and let steam for 1 minute, or until tender. Stir in the cooked rice and the plum, chilli and soy sauces. Set aside for about 20 minutes to cool.

Preheat the oven to 190°C (375°F/Gas 5). Remove two sheets of pastry, keeping the remaining pastry covered with a damp tea towel (dish towel). Place one sheet on top of the other, brush the edges with a little water, then scatter some breadcrumbs over the pastry. Top with two sheets of pastry, fold over the edges to make a 2 cm (3/4 inch) border and brush with a little water. Press the edges down with your fingertips.

Place one-quarter of the filling 5 cm (2 inches) from the short end, then firmly roll into a parcel to encase the filling, ensuring that the seam is underneath. Repeat with the remaining ingredients. Brush the tops lightly with butter, cut three slashes across the top of each parcel and scatter any remaining breadcrumbs and the sesame seeds over the top. Bake on a greased baking tray for 20–25 minutes, or until crisp and golden. Serve immediately, drizzled with sweet chilli sauce.

pasta napolitana

1 tablespoon olive oil
1 onion, finely chopped
1 carrot, finely chopped
1 celery stalk, finely chopped
500 g (1 lb 2 oz) ripe tomatoes, chopped
2 tablespoons chopped parsley
2 teaspoons sugar
500 g (1 lb 2 oz) pasta (see Note)

serves 6

method Heat the oil in a heavy-based saucepan. Add the onion, carrot and celery. Cover and cook over low heat for 10 minutes, stirring occasionally.

Add the tomato to the vegetables with the parsley, sugar and 125 ml (4 fl oz/½ cup) water. Bring to the boil, reduce the heat to low, cover and simmer for 45 minutes, stirring occasionally. Season with salt and pepper. If necessary, add a little more water to thin the sauce.

Add the pasta to a large saucepan of rapidly boiling salted water and cook until al dente. Drain and then return to the pan. Pour the sauce over the pasta and gently toss.

note *Traditionally, spaghetti is used with this sauce, but you can use any pasta. The sauce can be reduced to a concentrated version by cooking it for a longer period. Store it in the refrigerator and add water or stock to thin it, if necessary, when reheating.*

stuffed eggplants

4 tablespoons brown lentils
2 large eggplants (aubergines)
cooking oil spray
1 red onion, chopped
2 garlic cloves, crushed
1 red capsicum (pepper), finely chopped
3 tablespoons pine nuts, toasted
140 g (5 oz/¾ cup) cooked short-grain rice
440 g (15 oz) tin chopped tomatoes
2 tablespoons chopped coriander (cilantro)
1 tablespoon chopped parsley
2 tablespoons grated parmesan cheese

serves 4

method Cook the brown lentils in a saucepan of simmering water for 25 minutes, or until soft, then drain. Cut the eggplants in half lengthways and scoop out the flesh, leaving a 1 cm (½ inch) shell. Chop the flesh finely.

Spray a large, deep non-stick frying pan with oil, add 1 tablespoon water, then add the onion and garlic and stir until softened. Add the cooked lentils to the pan with the capsicum, pine nuts, rice, tomato and eggplant flesh. Stir over medium heat for 10 minutes, or until the eggplant has softened. Add the fresh coriander and parsley. Season, then toss until well mixed.

Cook the eggplant shells in boiling water for 4–5 minutes, or until just tender. Spoon the filling into the shells and sprinkle with the parmesan. Grill (broil) for 5–10 minutes, or until golden. Serve immediately.

vegetable curry

250 g (9 oz) potatoes, peeled and diced
250 g (9 oz) pumpkin (winter squash), peeled
   and diced
200 g (7 oz) cauliflower, broken into florets
150 g (5 oz) yellow squash, cut into quarters
1 tablespoon oil
2 onions, chopped
3 tablespoons curry powder
400 g (14 oz) tin chopped tomatoes
250 ml (9 fl oz/1 cup) vegetable stock
150 g (5 oz) green beans, cut into
   short lengths
4 tablespoons plain low-fat yoghurt
3 tablespoons sultanas (golden raisins)

serves 6

method   Bring a saucepan of water to the boil and cook the potato and pumpkin for 6 minutes, then remove. Add the cauliflower and squash, cook for 4 minutes, then remove.

Heat the oil in a large saucepan, add the onion and cook, stirring, over medium heat for 8 minutes, or until starting to brown. Add the curry powder and stir for 1 minute, or until fragrant. Stir in the tomato and stock. Add the potato, pumpkin, cauliflower and squash and cook for 5 minutes, then add the green beans and cook for a further 2–3 minutes, or until the vegetables are just tender.

Stir in the yoghurt and sultanas. Simmer for 3 minutes, or until thickened slightly. Season to taste and serve.

mushroom, ricotta and olive pizza

4 roma (plum) tomatoes, quartered
¾ teaspoon caster (superfine) sugar
10 g (¼ oz) dry yeast or 15 g (½ oz) fresh yeast
125 ml (4 fl oz/½ cup) skim milk
220 g (8 oz/1¾ cups) plain (all-purpose) flour
2 teaspoons olive oil
2 garlic cloves, crushed
1 onion, thinly sliced
750 g (1 lb 10 oz) mushrooms, sliced
250 g (9 oz/1 cup) low-fat ricotta cheese
2 tablespoons sliced black olives
small handful basil leaves

serves 6

method   Preheat the oven to 210°C (415°F/Gas 6–7). Put the tomato on a baking tray covered with baking paper, sprinkle with salt, cracked black pepper and ½ teaspoon sugar and bake for 20 minutes, or until the edges are starting to darken.

Stir the yeast and remaining sugar with 3 tablespoons warm water until the yeast dissolves. Cover and leave in a warm place until foamy. Warm the milk. Sift the flour into a large bowl and stir in the yeast and milk. Mix to a soft dough, then turn onto a lightly floured surface and knead for 5 minutes. Leave, covered, in a lightly oiled bowl in a warm place for 40 minutes, or until doubled in size.

Heat the oil in a frying pan and fry the garlic and onion until soft. Add the mushrooms and stir until they are soft and the liquid has evaporated. Leave to cool.

Turn the dough out onto a lightly floured surface and knead lightly. Roll out to a 38 cm (15 inch) circle and transfer to a lightly greased oven or pizza tray. Spread with the ricotta, leaving a border to turn over the filling. Top with the mushrooms, leaving a circle in the centre. Arrange the tomato and olives in the circle. Fold the dough edge over onto the mushroom and dust the edge with flour. Bake for 25 minutes, or until the crust is golden. Garnish with basil.

silverbeet parcels

500 ml (17 fl oz/2 cups) vegetable stock
1 tablespoon olive oil
1 onion, chopped
2 garlic cloves, crushed
1 red capsicum (pepper), chopped
250 g (9 oz) mushrooms, chopped
110 g (4 oz/½ cup) arborio rice
60 g (2 oz/½ cup) grated low-fat cheddar
  cheese
1 large handful shredded basil
6 large silverbeet (Swiss chard) leaves
2 x 400 g (14 oz) tins chopped tomatoes
1 tablespoon balsamic vinegar
1 teaspoon soft brown sugar

serves 6

method   Heat the stock in a saucepan and maintain at simmering point. Heat the oil in a large saucepan and cook the onion and garlic until the onion has softened. Add the capsicum, mushrooms and rice and stir until well combined. Gradually add 125 ml (4 fl oz/½ cup) hot stock, stirring until the liquid has been absorbed. Continue to add the stock, a little at a time, until it has all been absorbed and the rice is tender. Remove from the heat, add the cheese and basil and season to taste.

Trim the stalks from the silverbeet and cook the leaves, a few at a time, in a large saucepan of boiling water for 30 seconds, or until wilted. Drain on a tea towel (dish towel). Using a sharp knife, cut away any tough white veins from the centre of the leaves. Place a portion of mushroom filling in the centre of each leaf, fold in the sides and roll up carefully. Tie with string.

Put the tomato, balsamic vinegar and brown sugar in a large, deep non-stick frying pan and stir to combine. Add the silverbeet parcels, cover and simmer for 10 minutes. Remove the string and serve with tomato sauce.

fettuccine boscaiola

500 g (1 lb 2 oz) button mushrooms
1 large onion
1 tablespoon olive oil
2 garlic cloves, finely chopped
2 x 425 g (15 oz) tins tomatoes, chopped
500 g (1 lb 2 oz) fettuccine
2 tablespoons chopped parsley

serves 6

method   Wipe the mushrooms with a damp paper towel and then slice finely, including the stems.

Chop the onion roughly. Heat the oil in a heavy-based frying pan and cook the onion and garlic over medium heat, stirring occasionally, for about 6 minutes, or until the vegetables are light golden. Add the tomato including the juice, along with the mushrooms, to the pan and bring the mixture to the boil. Reduce the heat, cover the pan and simmer for 15 minutes.

While the sauce is cooking, cook the fettuccine in a large saucepan of rapidly boiling salted water until al dente. Drain and return to the pan.

Stir the parsley into the sauce and season well with salt and pepper. Toss the sauce through the pasta.

spinach pie

1.5 kg (3 lb 5 oz) English spinach
2 teaspoons olive oil
1 onion, chopped
4 spring onions (scallions), chopped
750 g (1 lb 10 oz/3 cups) low-fat cottage
   cheese
2 eggs, lightly beaten
2 garlic cloves, crushed
pinch of ground nutmeg
1 large handful mint, chopped
8 sheets filo pastry
30 g (1 oz) butter, melted
40 g (1½ oz/½ cup) fresh breadcrumbs

serves 6

method   Preheat the oven to 180°C (350°F/Gas 4). Lightly spray a 1.5 litre (52 fl oz/6 cup) capacity ovenproof dish with oil. Trim and wash the spinach, then place in a large saucepan. Cover and cook for 2–3 minutes, until the spinach has just wilted. Drain, cool then squeeze dry and chop.

Heat the oil in a small pan. Add the onion and spring onion and cook for 2–3 minutes, until softened. Combine in a bowl with the chopped spinach. Stir in the cottage cheese, egg, garlic, nutmeg and mint. Season and mix together well.

Brush a sheet of filo pastry with a little butter. Fold in half widthways and line the base and sides of the dish. Repeat with three more sheets. Keep the unused sheets moist by covering with a damp tea towel (dish towel).

Sprinkle the breadcrumbs over the pastry. Spread the filling into the dish. Fold over any overlapping pastry. Brush and fold another sheet and place on top. Repeat with 3 more sheets. Tuck the pastry in at the sides. Brush the top with the remaining butter. Score diamonds on top using a sharp knife. Bake for 40 minutes, or until golden. Cut the pie into squares to serve.

chickpea curry

220 g (8 oz/1 cup) dried chickpeas
1 tablespoon oil
2 onions, finely chopped
2 large ripe tomatoes, chopped
½ teaspoon ground coriander
1 teaspoon ground cumin
1 teaspoon chilli powder
¼ teaspoon ground turmeric
1 tablespoon channa masala (see Note)
1 small white onion, sliced
mint and coriander leaves, to garnish

serves 6

method   Place the chickpeas in a bowl, cover with water and leave to soak overnight. Drain, rinse and place in a large saucepan. Cover with plenty of water and bring to the boil, then reduce the heat and simmer for 40 minutes, or until soft. Drain.

Heat the oil in a large saucepan, add the onion and cook over medium heat for 15 minutes, until golden brown. Add the chopped tomato, ground coriander and cumin, chilli powder, turmeric, channa masala and 500 ml (17 fl oz/2 cups) water and cook for 10 minutes, or until the tomato is soft.

Add the chickpeas, season and cook for 7–10 minutes, or until the sauce thickens. Garnish with sliced onion and fresh mint and coriander leaves.

note   *Channa (chole) masala is a spice blend available at Indian grocery stores. Garam masala can be used as a substitute but the flavour will be a little different.*

layered country cob

2 red capsicums (peppers)
1 eggplant (aubergine), thinly sliced
1 large red onion, thinly sliced
450 g (1 lb) white cob loaf
1 tablespoon olive oil
2 garlic cloves, finely chopped
1 teaspoon chopped lemon thyme
250 g (9 oz) English spinach
350 g (12 oz) ricotta cheese

serves 8

method   Preheat the grill (broiler) to hot. Cut the capsicum in quarters lengthways and remove the seeds and membrane. Arrange the capsicum, skin side up, and the eggplant, sprayed lightly with oil, on the grill. Grill (broil) for about 7 minutes, turning the eggplant over as it browns and until the capsicum skin is blackened and blistered, then leave to cool. Grill the onion for about 6 minutes, turning once, until softened. Peel the skin away from the capsicum.

Cut the top off the cob and pull out the centre. Combine the oil, garlic and thyme and brush lightly inside the shell. Put the spinach leaves in a bowl and pour boiling water over to cover. Allow to soften for 1 minute, rinse with cold water until cool, then drain and pat dry with paper towels.

To fill the cob, arrange half the eggplant in the base, followed by capsicum and onion, then a layer of ricotta, spinach and the remaining eggplant. Season between layers. Press down firmly. If the top of the cob is empty, fill the space with a little of the soft bread from the centre. Replace the top of the loaf and wrap the whole thing securely with foil. Top with a brick wrapped in foil, or a heavy bowl to weigh it down. Refrigerate overnight. Cut into wedges to serve.

potato gnocchi with tomato sauce

500 g (1 lb 2 oz) floury potatoes, unpeeled
1 egg yolk
3 tablespoons grated parmesan cheese,
plus extra, to serve
125 g (5 oz/1 cup) plain (all-purpose) flour

tomato sauce

425 g (15 oz) tin tomatoes, chopped
1 small onion, chopped
1 celery stalk, chopped
1 small carrot, chopped
1 tablespoon shredded basil
1 teaspoon chopped thyme
1 garlic clove, crushed
1 teaspoon caster (superfine) sugar

serves 4

method Steam or boil the potatoes until just tender. Drain thoroughly and set aside to cool for 10 minutes before peeling and mashing them.

Measure 2 cups of the mashed potato into a large bowl, mix in the egg yolk, parmesan, $1/4$ teaspoon of salt and some black pepper. Slowly add the flour until you have a slightly sticky dough. Knead for 5 minutes, adding more flour if necessary, until a smooth dough is formed.

Divide the dough into four portions and roll each on a lightly floured surface to form a sausage shape, about 2 cm ($3/4$ inch) thick. Cut the rolls into 2.5 cm (1 inch) slices and shape each piece into an oval. Press each oval into the palm of your hand against a floured fork, to flatten slightly and indent one side with a pattern. As you make the gnocchi place them in a single layer on a baking tray and cover until ready to use.

To make the tomato sauce, mix all the ingredients with salt and pepper in a saucepan. Bring to the boil, reduce the heat to low–medium and simmer for 30 minutes, stirring occasionally. Allow to cool, then process in a food processor or blender, until smooth. Reheat if necessary before serving.

Cook the gnocchi in batches in a large saucepan of boiling salted water for 2 minutes, or until they float to the surface. Drain well. Serve the gnocchi tossed through the sauce, sprinkled with parmesan.

vegetarian chilli

150 g (5 oz/¾ cup) burghul (bulgur)
1 tablespoon olive oil
1 large onion, finely chopped
2 garlic cloves, crushed
1 teaspoon chilli powder
2 teaspoons ground cumin
1 teaspoon cayenne pepper
½ teaspoon ground cinnamon
2 x 400 g (14 oz) tins chopped tomatoes
750 ml (26 fl oz/3 cups) vegetable stock
440 g (15 oz) tin red kidney beans, drained
    and rinsed
2 x 300 g (11 oz) tins chickpeas, drained
    and rinsed
310 g (11 oz) tin corn kernels, drained
2 tablespoons tomato paste
    (concentrated purée)
corn chips and light sour cream, for serving

serves 8

method   Soak the burghul in 250 ml (9 fl oz/1 cup) hot water for 10 minutes. Heat the oil in a heavy-based saucepan and cook the onion for 10 minutes, stirring often, until soft and golden.

Add the garlic, chilli powder, cumin, cayenne and cinnamon and cook, stirring, for a further minute.

Add the tomato, stock and burghul. Bring to the boil and simmer for 10 minutes. Stir in the kidney beans, chickpeas, corn and tomato paste and simmer for 20 minutes, stirring often. Serve with corn chips and sour cream.

note   *Chilli will keep for up to 3 days in the refrigerator (and can be frozen for up to 1 month).*

roast vegetable quiche

cooking oil spray
1 large potato
400 g (14 oz) pumpkin (winter squash)
200 g (7 oz) orange sweet potato
2 large parsnips
1 red capsicum (pepper)
2 onions, cut into wedges
6 garlic cloves, halved
2 teaspoons olive oil
150 g (5 oz/1¼ cups) plain (all-purpose) flour
40 g (1½ oz) butter
40 g (1½ oz) ricotta cheese
250 ml (9 fl oz/1 cup) skim milk
3 eggs, lightly beaten
3 tablespoons grated low-fat cheddar cheese
2 tablespoons chopped basil

serves 6

method Preheat the oven to 180°C (350°F/Gas 4). Lightly spray a 3 cm (1¼ inch) deep, 23 cm (9 inch) diameter loose-based flan (tart) tin with oil. Cut the potato, pumpkin, sweet potato, parsnips and capsicum into bite-sized chunks, place in a baking dish with the onion and garlic and drizzle with the oil. Season and bake for 1 hour, or until the vegetables are tender. Leave to cool.

Mix the flour, butter and ricotta in a food processor, then gradually add up to 3 tablespoons of the milk, enough to form a soft dough. Turn out onto a lightly floured surface and gather together into a smooth ball. Cover and refrigerate for 15 minutes.

Roll the pastry out on a lightly floured surface, then ease into the tin. Trim the edge and refrigerate for another 10 minutes. Increase the oven to 200°C (400°F/Gas 6). Cover the pastry with crumpled baking paper and fill with baking beads or uncooked rice. Bake for 10 minutes, remove the beads or rice and paper, then bake for another 10 minutes, or until golden brown.

Place the vegetables in the pastry base and then pour in the combined remaining milk, eggs, cheese and basil. Reduce the oven temperature to 180°C (350°F/Gas 4) and bake for 1 hour 10 minutes, or until set in the centre. Leave for 5 minutes before removing from the tin to serve.

sweet things

fruit tarts

125 g (4½ oz/1 cup) plain (all-purpose) flour
3 tablespoons custard powder
3 tablespoons icing (confectioners') sugar
40 g (1½ oz) butter
2 tablespoons low-fat milk
2 x 130 g (5 oz) tubs low-fat strawberry
    fromage frais
100 g (4 oz) ricotta cheese
halved strawberries, blueberries, kiwi fruit,
    peeled and sliced
2 tablespoons apricot jam

serves 8

method Grease eight 7 cm (2¾ inch) loose-based flan (tart) tins. Mix the flour, custard powder, icing sugar and butter in a food processor until fine crumbs form, then add enough of the milk to form a soft dough. Gather into a ball, wrap in plastic and chill for 30 minutes.

Preheat the oven to 200°C (400°F/Gas 6). Divide the dough into eight portions and roll out to line the tins. Cover with paper and rice or dried beans. Bake for 10 minutes, remove the paper and rice and bake for another 10 minutes, or until golden. Cool and remove from the tins.

Mix the fromage frais and ricotta until smooth. Spread over the pastry bases and top with assorted fruit. Heat the jam until liquid, then brush over the fruit to glaze.

mango and passionfruit sorbet

250 g (9 oz/1 cup) caster (superfine) sugar
4 tablespoons passionfruit pulp
½ large mango, about 200 g (7 oz), chopped
1 large peach, about 250 g (9 oz), chopped
2 tablespoons lemon juice
1 egg white

serves 6

method Stir the sugar in a saucepan with 250 ml (9 fl oz/1 cup) water over low heat until dissolved. Increase the heat, bring to the boil and boil for 1 minute. Transfer to a glass bowl, cool, then refrigerate. Strain the passionfruit pulp, reserving 1 tablespoon of the seeds.

Blend the fruit, passionfruit juice and lemon juice in a blender until smooth. With the motor running, add the cold sugar syrup and 150 ml (5 fl oz) water. Stir in the passionfruit seeds. Freeze in a shallow container, stirring occasionally, for about 5 hours, or until almost set.

Break up the icy mixture with a fork or spoon, transfer to a bowl and beat with electric beaters until smooth and fluffy. Beat the egg white in a small bowl until firm peaks form, then fold into the mixture until just combined. Spread into a loaf tin and then return to the freezer until firm. Transfer to the refrigerator, to soften, 15 minutes before serving.

variation *To make a berry sorbet, use 200 g (7 oz) blackberries or blueberries, 200 g (7 oz) hulled strawberries and 50 g (2 oz) peach flesh. Prepare as above.*

brazil nut and coffee biscotti

3 teaspoons instant coffee powder
1 tablespoon dark rum, warmed
2 eggs
125 g (4½ oz/½ cup) caster (superfine) sugar
155 g (5½ oz/1¼ cups) plain (all-purpose) flour
60 g (2 oz/½ cup) self-raising flour
1 teaspoon ground cinnamon
105 g (3½ oz/¾ cup) Brazil nuts,
    roughly chopped
1 tablespoon caster (superfine) sugar, extra

makes 40

method   Preheat the oven to 180°C (350°F/Gas 4). Dissolve the coffee in the rum. Beat the eggs and sugar until thick and creamy, then beat in the coffee. Sift the flours and cinnamon into a bowl, then stir in the nuts. Mix in the egg mixture.

Divide the mixture into two rolls, each about 28 cm (11¼ inches) long. Line a baking tray with baking paper, put the rolls on it and press lightly to flatten to about 6 cm (2½ inches) across. Brush lightly with water and sprinkle with the extra sugar. Bake for 25 minutes, or until firm and light brown. Cool until warm on the tray. Reduce the oven temperature to 160°C (315°F/Gas 2–3).

Cut into 1 cm (½ inch) thick diagonal slices. Bake in a single layer on the lined tray for 20 minutes, until dry, turning once. Cool on a rack. When cold, these can be stored in an airtight container for 2–3 weeks.

figs with orange cream and raisins

150 g (5 oz/1¼ cups) raisins
4 tablespoons tawny port
1 tablespoon custard powder
250 ml (9 fl oz/1 cup) skim milk
1 tablespoon sugar
100 g (4 oz) ricotta cheese
200 g (7 oz) low-fat fromage frais
zest strips and juice of 1 orange
1 teaspoon ground cinnamon
8 fresh figs

serves 4

method   Soak the raisins in the tawny port for 1 hour, or until plumped up.

Blend the custard powder with the skim milk in a small saucepan. Add the sugar and stir over low heat until dissolved. Increase the heat and stir until the custard boils and thickens. Remove from the heat immediately, pour into a small bowl and cover with plastic wrap. Cool completely. Transfer to an electric mixer, add the ricotta and fromage frais and beat until smooth.

Warm the raisin mixture with the orange zest, juice and cinnamon in a small saucepan. Cover and keep warm.

Starting from the top, cut the figs into quarters, slicing only two-thirds of the way down so they hold together. Transfer to ramekins or a serving dish or platter. Place 2 heaped tablespoons of the custard cream mixture into the centre of each fig, top with a spoonful of the warm raisin and orange mixture and serve at once.

meringue baskets with fruit

2 egg whites
small pinch cream of tartar
125 g (4½ oz/½ cup) caster (superfine) sugar
2 tablespoons custard powder
500 ml (17 fl oz/2 cups) skim milk
1 teaspoon natural vanilla extract
1 peach, cut into thin wedges
1 kiwi fruit, cut into thin wedges
6 strawberries, cut in half
2 tablespoons apricot jam

serves 6

method   Preheat the oven to low 150°C (300°F/Gas 2) and line a baking tray with baking paper. Beat the egg whites and cream of tartar with electric beaters until soft peaks form. Gradually add the sugar and beat until it is dissolved and the mixture is stiff and glossy.

Fit a piping bag with a medium star nozzle and pipe coiled spirals of the meringue (about 7.5 cm/ 3 inches) onto the tray. Pipe an extra ring around the top edge to make baskets. Bake for 30 minutes, then reduce the heat to 120°C (235°F/Gas ½). Bake for 45 minutes, turn the oven off and cool with the oven door ajar.

Mix the custard powder with a little of the milk to form a smooth paste. Transfer to a saucepan with the remaining milk and the vanilla essence. Stir over medium heat until the mixture boils and thickens. Remove from the heat and place plastic wrap over the surface to stop a skin forming. Set aside and, when cool, stir until smooth. Spoon some of the cold custard into each basket. Top with fruit. Heat the jam until liquid, then brush over the fruit to glaze.

berries in champagne jelly

1 litre (35 fl oz/4 cups) Champagne or
sparkling white wine
1½ tablespoons gelatine
250 g (9 oz/1 cup) sugar
4 strips lemon zest
4 strips orange zest
250 g (9 oz/1⅔ cups) small
strawberries, hulled
250 g (9 oz/1⅔ cups) blueberries

serves 8

method Pour 500 ml (17 fl oz/2 cups) Champagne or sparkling white wine into a bowl and let the bubbles subside. Sprinkle the gelatine over the top in an even layer. Leave until the gelatine is spongy; do not stir. Place the remaining Champagne in a large saucepan with the sugar, lemon and orange zest and heat gently, stirring, until all the sugar has dissolved.

Remove the pan from the heat, add the gelatine mixture and stir until thoroughly dissolved. Leave the jelly to cool completely, then remove the lemon and orange zest.

Divide the strawberries and blueberries among eight 125 ml (4 fl oz/½ cup) glasses or bowls and pour the jelly over them. Chill until the jelly has fully set. Remove from the fridge 15 minutes before serving.

banana pancakes

2 very ripe bananas, mashed
150 g (5½ oz/1 cup) wholemeal
   (whole-wheat) flour
2 teaspoons baking powder
½ teaspoon ground cinnamon
pinch ground nutmeg
250 ml (9 fl oz/1 cup) skim milk
1 tablespoon maple syrup
cooking oil spray
maple syrup and banana, for serving

serves 10

method   Put the mashed banana in a large bowl. Sift the flour, baking powder, cinnamon and nutmeg onto the banana and return the husks to the bowl. Stir until the flour is moistened but not totally combined with the mashed banana.

Make a well in the centre, add the milk and maple syrup and stir constantly until smooth. Set aside for 1 hour.

Heat a large non-stick frying pan over medium heat and coat with oil spray. Cook the pancakes in batches, using 3 tablespoons of batter for each pancake. Cook for 3–4 minutes, or until small bubbles appear on the surface. Using a spatula, turn the pancakes over, loosening the edges first so they don't stick to the pan. Cook for another 3 minutes. Remove from the pan and keep warm. Spray the pan with a little oil after each batch and continue with the remaining mixture. Serve drizzled with maple syrup and a few slices of banana.

pears poached in dark grape juice

6 beurre bosc (or any firm) pears
2 tablespoons lemon juice
500 ml (17 fl oz/2 cups) dark grape juice
500 ml (17 fl oz/2 cups) blackcurrant juice
2 tablespoons sweet sherry
4 cloves
350 g (12 oz) black grapes
250 g (9 oz/1 cup) low-fat plain yoghurt
½ teaspoon ground cinnamon
1 tablespoon honey

serves 6

method   Core and peel the pears, leaving the stalks on. Place the pears, as you peel, in a bowl filled with cold water and the lemon juice, to prevent browning.

Put the grape and blackcurrant juices, sherry and cloves in a saucepan large enough to hold the pears. Add the pears.

Bring the liquid to the boil, then reduce to a simmer. Cover and cook for 35–40 minutes, or until tender. Remove from the heat and leave the pears to cool in the syrup. Transfer the pears and syrup to a bowl and cover with plastic wrap. Refrigerate overnight.

To serve, strain the syrup into a saucepan and bring to the boil, then reduce to a simmer and cook for 40 minutes, or until reduced by about two-thirds. Cool slightly, then put a pear on each plate and pour syrup over the pears. Arrange the grapes next to the pears. Just before serving, mix the yoghurt with the cinnamon and honey and spoon over the pears or serve on the side.

passionfruit tart

90 g (3 oz/¾ cup) plain (all-purpose) flour
2 tablespoons icing (confectioners') sugar
2 tablespoons custard powder
30 g (1 oz) butter
3 tablespoons light evaporated milk

filling

125 g (5 oz/½ cup) ricotta cheese
1 teaspoon natural vanilla extract
3 tablespoons icing (confectioners') sugar,
  plus extra, for dusting
2 eggs, lightly beaten
4 tablespoons passionfruit pulp
  (about 8 passionfruit)
185 ml (6 fl oz/¾ cup) light evaporated milk

serves 8

method   Preheat the oven to 200°C (400°F/Gas 6). Lightly spray a 23 cm (9 inch) loose-based flan (tart) tin with oil. Sift the flour, icing sugar and custard powder into a bowl and rub in the butter until crumbs form. Add enough evaporated milk to form a soft dough. Bring together on a floured surface until just smooth. Gather into a ball, wrap in plastic and chill for 15 minutes.

Roll the pastry out on a floured surface to fit the tin, then refrigerate for a further 15 minutes. Cover with baking paper and fill with rice or dried beans. Bake for 10 minutes, then remove the rice or beans and paper and bake for another 5–8 minutes, or until golden. Allow to cool. Reduce the oven to 160°C (315°F/Gas 2–3).

Beat the ricotta with the vanilla essence and icing sugar until smooth. Add the eggs, passionfruit pulp and evaporated milk, then beat well. Put the tin with the pastry case on a baking tray and pour in the filling. Bake for 40 minutes, or until set. Cool in the tin. Dust with icing sugar to serve, if desired.

raspberry mousse

3 teaspoons gelatine
250 g (9 oz/1 cup) low-fat vanilla yoghurt
2 x 200 g (7 oz) tubs low-fat fromage frais
4 egg whites
150 g (5 oz) raspberries, mashed
extra raspberries and mint leaves, for serving

serves 4

method   Sprinkle the gelatine in an even layer onto 1 tablespoon water in a small bowl and leave to go spongy. Bring a small saucepan of water to the boil, remove from the heat and place the bowl in the pan. Stir until clear.

In a large bowl, stir the vanilla yoghurt and fromage frais together, then add the gelatine and mix well.

Using electric beaters, beat the egg whites until stiff peaks form, then fold through the yoghurt mixture. Transfer half to a separate bowl and fold the mashed raspberries through.

Divide the raspberry mixture into the bases of four long glasses or serving bowls. Top with the vanilla mixture. Refrigerate for several hours, or until set. Decorate with fresh raspberries and mint leaves.

almond and pear crêpes

4 beurre bosc (or any firm) pears
3 tablespoons dry white wine
3 tablespoons caster (superfine) sugar
1 cinnamon stick
2 cloves
1 vanilla bean
4 dates, roughly chopped
2 tablespoons sultanas (golden raisins)
85 g (3 oz/⅔ cup) plain (all-purpose) flour
1 egg, lightly beaten
250 ml (9 fl oz/1 cup) skim milk
cooking oil spray
2 tablespoons ground almonds
1 tablespoon soft brown sugar
½ teaspoon ground cinnamon
2 teaspoons flaked almonds
icing (confectioners') sugar, for dusting

strawberry sauce

125 g (5 oz) strawberries, chopped
1 teaspoon caster (superfine) sugar
2 tablespoons orange juice

serves 4

method Remove the cores of the pears using a melon baller, then peel the pears. Combine 500 ml (17 fl oz/2 cups) water with the wine, sugar, cinnamon stick and cloves in a saucepan large enough to fit the pears. Split the bean in half lengthways and scrape the seeds out. Add the seeds to the pan with the bean and stir over medium heat until the sugar has dissolved. Add the pears and simmer, covered, for about 20 minutes. Remove from the heat and allow to cool in the syrup. Drain and stand the pears on paper towels. Fill the base of each with the dates and sultanas.

To make the crêpes, sift the flour into a bowl, gradually beat in the egg and milk, beating until smooth. Strain into a bowl and set aside for 10 minutes. Preheat the oven to 200°C (400°F/Gas 6). Lightly oil a 24 cm (9½ inch) non-stick frying pan with oil spray, heat the pan and pour in a quarter of the batter, swirling to cover the base of the pan. Cook until lightly browned, then turn and brown the other side. Remove and repeat with the remaining mixture.

Place the crêpes on a work surface, place a quarter of the ground almonds, brown sugar and cinnamon in the centre of each crêpe and top with a pear. Gather the crêpes around the pears and tie with string. Sprinkle with the flaked almonds. Bake on a lightly oiled baking tray for 5 minutes. Discard the string.

To make the strawberry sauce, blend all the ingredients in a blender until smooth and then strain. Dust the pear crêpes with icing sugar and serve with strawberry sauce.

watermelon and vodka granita

1 kg (2 lb 4 oz) piece of watermelon, rind
removed (to leave 600 g/1 lb 5 oz)
2 teaspoons lime juice
3 tablespoons caster (superfine) sugar
3 tablespoons citrus-flavoured vodka

serves 6

method Coarsely chop the watermelon, removing the seeds. Place the flesh in a food processor and add the lime juice and sugar. Process until smooth, then strain through a fine sieve. Stir in the vodka, then taste—if the watermelon is not very sweet, you may have to add a little more sugar.

Pour into a shallow 1.5 litre (6 cup) metal tin and freeze for about 1 hour, or until beginning to freeze around the edges. Scrape the frozen parts back into the mixture with a fork. Repeat every 30 minutes for another 4 hours, or until even ice crystals have formed.

Beat with a fork just before serving. To serve, scrape into dishes with a fork.

hint *A scoop of the granita in a shot glass with vodka is great for summer cocktail parties.*

chestnut hearts

150 g (5½ oz/⅔ cup) caster (superfine) sugar
2 eggs
2½ teaspoons coconut essence
6 egg whites
1 teaspoon cream of tartar
155 g (5½ oz/1¼ cups) self-raising flour, sifted
250 g (9 oz/1 cup) tinned sweetened chestnut
  purée
4 tablespoons ricotta cheese
2 teaspoons cocoa powder
icing (confectioners') sugar, to dust

serves 4

method   Preheat the oven to 180°C (350°F/ Gas 4). Lightly spray two 20 x 30 cm (8 x 12 inch) shallow baking tins with oil and line with baking paper.

Beat the sugar and eggs in a bowl with electric beaters for 3–4 minutes, until light and fluffy. Transfer to a large bowl. Add the coconut essence.

Beat the egg whites until foamy. Add the cream of tartar and beat until firm peaks form. Stir a third of the egg white into the creamed mixture. Slowly fold in the flour in small batches, alternating with small amounts of egg white. Fold in both until just combined. Divide the mixture between the trays. Bake for 20–25 minutes, until golden. Test with a skewer. Turn out onto cooling racks lined with baking paper. Leave until completely cold (if possible, make a day in advance).

In a blender, mix the chestnut purée with the ricotta and cocoa until very smooth. Slice the cakes in half horizontally and join with the chestnut mixture. Cut out heart shapes using a 5 cm (2 inch) heart-shaped cookie cutter. Clean the cutter between cuts or dust it in icing sugar if the cake sticks. Dust with icing sugar before serving.

passionfruit bavarois

2 x 170 g (6 oz) tins passionfruit in syrup
300 g (11 oz) silken tofu, chopped
600 ml (21 fl oz) buttermilk
2 tablespoons caster (superfine) sugar
1 teaspoon natural vanilla extract
2½ tablespoons gelatine
185 ml (6 fl oz/¾ cup) passionfruit pulp

serves 4

method Push the passionfruit in syrup through a sieve. Discard the seeds. Combine the strained syrup with the tofu, buttermilk, caster sugar and vanilla in a blender. Blend for 90 seconds on high, to mix thoroughly. Leave in the blender.

Put 4 tablespoons water in a small bowl and put the bowl in a slightly larger bowl of boiling water. Sprinkle the gelatine onto the water in the small bowl and stir until dissolved. Leave to cool.

Place eight 200 ml (7 fl oz) dariole moulds in a baking dish. Add the gelatine to the blender and mix on high for 1 minute. Pour into the moulds, cover the dish with plastic wrap and refrigerate overnight.

When ready to serve, carefully run a spatula around the edge of each mould and dip the bases in hot water for 2 seconds to make removal easier. Unmould each bavarois onto a plate and spoon the passionfruit pulp over the top and around the bases.

strawberry and banana ice

300 g (11 oz) silken tofu, chopped
250 g (9 oz) strawberries, chopped
2 ripe bananas, chopped
3 tablespoons caster (superfine) sugar

serves 4

method Blend the silken tofu, strawberries, banana and caster sugar in a blender or food processor, until smooth.

Pour the mixture into a shallow cake tin and freeze until almost frozen. Remove from the freezer and break up roughly with a fork or a spoon, then transfer to a large bowl and beat until it has a smooth texture. Pour the mixture evenly into a 15 x 25 cm (6 x 10 inch) loaf tin, cover and freeze again, until quite firm.

Alternatively, freeze the blended mixture in an ice cream machine until it is thick and creamy, then store in a covered container in the freezer.

Transfer to the refrigerator for about 30 minutes before serving to allow the ice to soften slightly.

fruit jellies

1 tablespoon gelatine
500 ml (17 fl oz/2 cups) cranberry and
raspberry juice
325 g (11 oz) mixed berries, fresh or frozen

serves 4

method   Sprinkle the gelatine in an even layer onto 3 tablespoons of the juice, in a small bowl, and leave to go spongy. Bring a small saucepan of water to the boil, remove from the heat and place the bowl in the pan. The water should come halfway up the side of the bowl. Stir until the gelatine is clear and has dissolved. Cool slightly and mix with the rest of the juice.

Rinse four 185 ml (6 fl oz/3/4 cup) moulds with water (wet moulds make it easier when unmoulding) and pour 2 cm (3/4 inch) of the juice into each. Refrigerate until set. Meanwhile, if the fruit is frozen, defrost it and add any liquid to the remaining juice. When the bottom layer of jelly has set, divide the fruit among the moulds (reserving a few berries to garnish) and then divide the rest of the juice among the moulds, pouring it over the fruit. Refrigerate until set.

To turn out the jellies, hold each mould in a hot, damp tea towel (dish towel) and turn out onto a plate. Ease away the edge of the jelly with your finger to break the seal. (If you turn the jellies onto a damp plate you will be able to move them around, otherwise they will stick.) Garnish with reserved berries.

126

Published in 2010 by Bay Books,
an imprint of Murdoch Books Pty Limited.

Murdoch Books Australia
Pier 8/9,
23 Hickson Road,
Millers Point NSW 2000
Phone: +61 (0)2 8220 2000
Fax: +61 (0)2 8220 2558
www.murdochbooks.com.au

Murdoch Books UK Limited
Erico House,
6th Floor North, 93–99 Upper Richmond Road,
Putney, London SW15 2TG
Phone: + 44 (0) 20 8785 5995
Fax: + 44 (0) 20 8785 5985
www.murdochbooks.co.uk

Chief Executive: Juliet Rogers

Publisher: Lynn Lewis
Senior Designer: Heather Menzies
Designer: Katy Wall
Editor: Justine Harding
Editorial Coordinator: Liz Malcolm
Index: Jo Rudd
Production: Alexandra Gonzalez

National Library of Australia Cataloguing-in-Publication Data:
Title: Light and easy.
ISBN: 978-1-74266-002-8 (pbk.)
Series: 100 easy recipes.
Notes: Includes index.
Subjects: Quick and easy cooking. Low-fat diet-recipes.
Dewey Number: 641.555

Printed by C & C Offset Printing Co. Ltd. PRINTED IN CHINA.